"America's health care reform can go either way.
It will either be the re-birth of the
primary care physician in America,
or it will crush the doctors."

— Peter B. Anderson, MD

THE
FAMILIAR
PHYSICIAN

Saving Your Doctor
In the Era of Obamacare

PETER B. ANDERSON, MD
WITH BUD RAMEY AND TOM EMSWILLER

NEW YORK

THE *Familiar Physician*
Saving Your Doctor In the Era of Obamacare

ISBN 978-1-61448-737-1 paperback
ISBN 978-1-61448-738-8 eBook
ISBN 978-1-61448-739-5 audio
Library of Congress Control Number: 2013945226

Morgan James Publishing
The Entrepreneurial Publisher
5 Penn Plaza, 23rd Floor,
New York City, New York 10001
(212) 655-5470 office • (516) 908-4496 fax
www.MorganJamesPublishing.com

Cover Design by:
Chris Treccani
www.3dogdesign.net

Interior Design by:
Bonnie Bushman
bonnie@caboodlegraphics.com

The following terms, appearing in this book, are registered or applied for trademarks of Team Care Medicine, LLC:

The *Familiar Physician* ™
Team Care Medicine™
Team Care ™

If you would like to contact the authors to order books, to arrange a public speaking engagement, or to discuss transformation training of your medical practice to our *Family Team Care* model, please do so at the following coordinates:

Dr. Peter Anderson
Team Care Medicine, LLC.
pandeson@teamcaremedicine.com
Telephone 757-650-5603
http://www.teamcaremedicine.org

In an effort to support local communities, raise awareness and funds, Morgan James Publishing donates a percentage of all book sales for the life of each book to Habitat for Humanity Peninsula and Greater Williamsburg.

Get involved today, visit
www.MorganJamesBuilds.com.

Habitat for Humanity®
Peninsula and
Greater Williamsburg
Building Partner

DEDICATION

To my wife, Laurie, who saw the possibilities
before they were obvious, the staff at Hilton
Family Practice who made those possibilities a
reality, and my family and friends who listened
and listened and listened...

The Familiar Physician —
Saving Your Doctor in the Era of Obamacare

Without the support of all of you,
this book would not be a reality.

Peter B. Anderson, MD

CONTENTS

**Part Five: The work continues to preserve
The *Familiar Physician*** 161

THE *FAMILIAR PHYSICIAN*

There are a number of factors that come together to create good medical care. One of the most important is the human connection that develops over time between a doctor and a patient. With the exception of a few clinical areas, the doctor-patient relationship is central, even essential, to the practice of medicine.

That's where the *Familiar Physician* comes in.

As a concept, the *Familiar Physician* represents a model of mutual trust and shared decision-making that strengthens and supports the diagnostic and therapeutic process. In fact, researchers have documented better outcomes for patients who have a primary care doctor as their ongoing source for care regardless of any demographic or health status differences.

But it's important to keep in mind that the *Familiar Physician* is more than just a concept. As a clinician ... as a person ... the *Familiar Physician* knows the patient well enough to identify a health issue better than a medical colleague who would be unfamiliar with the individual being treated. On the other side of the equation, the patient is comfortable enough to ask questions and confident that the doctor knows and cares about his or her personal values. No matter if the connection is formal, casual or somewhere in between, it's a partnership that will always be more effective when people are familiar with each other.

For health care reform to reach its ultimate goals it will, by necessity, travel through the field of primary care. And for primary care to fulfill its promise in the overall area of medicine, there are a lot of very good reasons to hope that it will include the *Familiar Physician.*

*"The primary care doctors of America
do not know how powerful they are."*
—**Paul Grundy, MD**

*"By instituting proven reforms in their individual practices
to streamline operations, elevate nurses and escape their
time trap, primary care providers can reclaim their place as
the 'Familiar Physician', the first and best source for health
care for the vast majority of Americans."*
— **Peter B. Anderson, MD**

PART ONE

On a national level,
there are heroes here,
people who re-directed their lives
to make this change happen.

Not for a few months, but for a decade.
A crusade.

We can see that whatever form health care takes in the future it will, at the very least, contain the passion and inspiration they've already put into it.

There are moments in our life when we look back on things and suddenly realize when a watershed event happened.

Such it is for health care in America.

We are all facing the unknown. Few people really understand the new 2,000-page law related to health care reform, much less how it will affect us.

We didn't see this at the time, but a powerful series of events occurred, creating a key turning point.

And that turning point for our health care is the story of how two men rallied a thousand health care organizations and stakeholders around a new model of health care.

The *medical home.*

They didn't just rally a base of support. They rallied everyone. They didn't just rally doctors. They rallied large corporations, hospitals, pharmaceutical companies, politicians, federal officials, military medicine, Medicare, Medicaid, insurance companies, think tanks. Everybody.

Most of us missed these moments in our nation's delivery of health care, which will impact our family in ways we can only imagine for years to come.

The story of the *medical home* is an inspiring tale. Understanding how it came about helps us to view its importance to our future.

We can see how passion and inspiration are at the heart of what is to come to us from medicine in the future.

This is the story of two physicians who held up a vision high enough for others to see.

And of my struggle to help other family doctors meet the coming storm.

Drs. Martin Sepúlveda and Paul Grundy of IBM developed a strategy not to come up with the full shape of health care reform — only one vital piece.

They came up with a platform that would enable good medicine to thrive. Just the platform. Then they began to champion that idea.

The *medical home*. It's here. Or coming.

We can only hope our primary care doctors are ready for it. Because it can be a new beginning, or it could smother the *Familiar Physicians* we all want.

INTRODUCTION

Everything Depends on How Doctors
Respond to the Coming Perfect Storm

"In this pivotal period, a great deal depends on how
primary care doctors respond to the coming changes.
And much depends on how passionately the people who
receive, provide and manage health care advocate on behalf
of the Familiar Physician."
— Dr. Peter Anderson

In both my life and my work, I've found that sometimes, the best way to understand what something is may be to determine what it is not. Applying that model of reasoning to *The Familiar Physician*, this book is *not* an in-depth study of health policy and legislation. Similarly, it is *not* a comprehensive look at contemporary health care delivery, a collection of primary care case studies, a cautionary tale related to my personal story or the complete blueprint for building a better medical practice.

In fact, *The Familiar Physician* includes certain elements of all the above, but at its core, the book is a fervent reminder that business as usual is not an option for any of us.

For consumers of health care — and that includes health care providers along with everyone else — I'm gratified that you care enough about your health to pick up this book and learn more about the threats to primary care medicine. I urge you to share it with your primary care physician. You just might help make a difference in his or her career.

I am hopeful that this book has also found its way into the hands of many of my primary care physician colleagues. To you I want to convey my belief that despite the impending storm this is an extraordinarily good time to be practicing medicine, particularly in the area of primary care. I hope further that this book, to extend the meteorological metaphor a bit further, offers strategies to protect your practice, your patients, your staff and yourself from storm damage.

If you are in an administrative role within a primary care medical practice, a large multispecialty group practice or a health care organization thank you for recognizing the essential role of primary care providers and **thank you** for being open to new ideas on how to address the pressures being placed on primary care medicine and its practitioners.

What I would say to all of you is that while the current politicization of health care isn't likely to go away, adding to it on any level won't help improve the current state of primary care. Nor will it improve anyone's medical practice or anyone's health and quality of life.

For those who believe that the federal government doesn't have the particular skills needed to run something economically or efficiently, not to mention providing the special human touch needed with health care, you have some history to support your concerns. For those who believe that only the large-scale involvement of government can support our efforts to prevail in a crisis of national proportion, you have some precedence, too.

But either way, the train has left the station and treating health reform as a political football only impedes our ability to address the fundamental problems related to our personal health and the health care system.

In the midst of any contentious issue there's usually a simple truth, and the one contained within health care reform centers on the fact that the current system is not only unsustainable, it tends to trump the health of individuals with political and organizational interests.

Dr. Ted Epperly, who as president of the American Academy of Family Physicians carried the *medical home* message to the nation's policymakers, sees an upside to the discord in changing health care in America.

"The upside of that tension is that the magnitude of the storm can be told," he notes.

The good news is that some very dedicated, vocal and knowledgeable champions of primary care are doing their part to guide the way toward a reorganized health care system that will include improved delivery and reimbursement models such as the Patient-Centered Medical Home.

In this pivotal period, a great deal depends on how primary care doctors respond to the coming changes.

And much depends on how passionately the people who receive, provide and manage health care advocate on behalf of the *Familiar Physician*.

A DEDICATED DOCTOR TOILS LATE INTO THE NIGHT

Big Blue Awakens a Nation

The year is 2003. After a long day of seeing patients, a primary care physician continues working in his small office in Newport News, Virginia. Despite his hard work, his long hours and the experience he's gained in all the details of what it takes to be a successful family physician, he is struggling.

For Dr. Peter Anderson, little in his professional life seems to be going right. The medical practice he created twenty years before is in trouble. Recognizing the problem is bad enough. What's even worse is that he has no answers on how to make the situation better.

He's not able to see enough patients in a day to meet his increasing practice expenses, and he has less time for individual patients. It's getting more and more difficult to deal with the increasing complexity of insurance reimbursement. His employees are needing better pay and benefits.

The electronic medical record (EMR) he incorporated into the practice in 1998 seems to be costing more time than it's saving. Despite his time at the practice which normally ranges from ten to twelve hours, he's been bringing home charts, and sometimes getting up at 3 a.m. to finish the day's work.

He hasn't taken any time off in months and his most recent "vacation" was a medical mission.

Dr. Anderson is stressed and demoralized, feelings he shares with colleagues in 2003 as well as with many primary care practitioners now.

On the plus side he greatly enjoys the work itself and is dedicated to his patients. He has a rich and fulfilling personal life within a close and loving family. He has done reasonably well considering the inequities in compensation for primary care physicians. And up until the last few years, he's experienced numerous rewards beyond the compensation.

Up until the last few years.

But at this moment, this night in which a dedicated family doctor toils late into the night, the rewards seem few and distant. Right now, traveling back as we are to 2003, Dr. Anderson painfully admits to himself that he has lost most of the pleasure of practicing medicine. His patients aren't feeling the love either. Frustrated by the harried atmosphere, the unintended but all too frequent waiting and his growing lack of availability, one of them recently confided to a mutual friend that the office is "pretty much in chaos."

the office is "pretty much in chaos"

With the memory of that patient "review" fresh in his mind, Peter Anderson cuts off the lights to his office, walks to the parking area and drives home in the dark. As if to assure that his current state of mind won't improve on the ride, it's raining and cold.

As he watches the high beams intensify the raindrops, he wonders if he made a mistake in going into medicine. Or maybe it was specializing in primary care. As he questions his decision he thinks of other physicians, some very smart people among them, who are also straining to make their primary care practices viable.

This is not the world he imagined. With his children now grown into young adults and out of the home, this was to be the time he and Laurie enjoyed the benefits of their years of hard work … not the time when he would come home for dinner, eat quickly and then go back to work. He had become, as his wife painfully described, a "ghost" who moved in and out of their life together. The unyielding load of his professional life, as he confides to a close colleague, has overflowed into his personal life.

If there is any consolation in the bleak picture that continuously loops through his mind it's that the elevator has reached the basement. The situation is as bad as it can possibly get. Then his nurses notify him that they plan to leave.

"what's at stake is American medicine as we hoped it would be"

In the cartoons, a light bulb suddenly goes on over the character's head to indicate an idea. The ancient Greeks yelled out, "Eureka" when they had a flash of inspiration. The Zen Buddhists call this sudden breakthrough to wisdom "satori," and while Oprah didn't actually invent "the aha moment," she popularized it into a catch phrase.

On this rainy night, as he drives home exhausted and longing for a little sleep before crawling back onto the hamster wheel tomorrow, Dr. Peter Anderson has no such enlightenment. No light bulbs. No flashes. No special clarity.

But what he does have is a profound feeling that something has to change. Leaving his practice after twenty gratifying years is not an option. He will do whatever he has to do to improve the situation not only for himself, but for his family, his staff and his patients.

This is not the change itself, but it is the beginning of the hope that change may be possible. Though he still finds himself waking up during the night with concerns, he now keeps a pad of paper in the nightstand to write down ideas. He takes walks before going into the practice. He thinks about the problems from every angle he can imagine. And then he invents new angles.

He doesn't have a solution yet, he doesn't even have a strategy, but he begins taking the first steps on the road to change.

The journey itself will last nearly a decade.

to awaken a nation

In what might have seemed to Peter Anderson like a parallel universe, but was, in fact, taking place only a few hundred miles to the north and within a similar time period, two other dedicated physicians, both employed by IBM, were absorbed in the question of how primary care-based health systems could serve as an agent of change within the larger sphere of health care.

IBM's Dr. Martin Sepúlveda

The dysfunctional state of primary care and its consequences for U.S. businesses and their employees have been the focus for Dr. Martin Sepúlveda and Dr. Paul Grundy since they traced the high cost of IBM's health care tab to its "flat out inability to buy good preventive care or primary medicine."

Since then, both physicians have distinguished themselves as reform advocates on a global level and they have become national champions for a new care model that seeks to re-imagine the broken status quo: the Patient-Centered Medical Home (PCMH). The foundation of this approach is ensuring that each patient has an ongoing relationship with a primary care doctor.

"They didn't just rally a base of support. They rallied everyone. They didn't just rally doctors. They rallied large corporations, hospitals, pharmaceutical companies, politicians, federal officials, military medicine, Medicare, Medicaid, insurance companies, think tanks. Everybody."

The Commonwealth Fund, which has long been at the center of health policy and meaningful health care reform, notes that the real "Nirvana Moment" came when the two physicians realized that despite IBM's active participation in a handful of highly regarded pay-for-performance efforts, they still hadn't been able to address employees' concerns around the core issues of access, convenience, and personalized attention that are key to meaningful and clinically-effective relationships between doctors and patients.

IBM's Dr. Paul Grundy

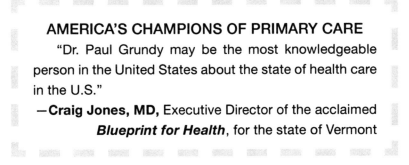

AMERICA'S CHAMPIONS OF PRIMARY CARE

"Dr. Paul Grundy may be the most knowledgeable person in the United States about the state of health care in the U.S."

—**Craig Jones, MD,** Executive Director of the acclaimed ***Blueprint for Health***, for the state of Vermont

As a world leader in information technology and consulting, IBM had helped create the tools that have enabled health care organizations to improve efficiencies and quality of care as part of a transition to more predictive patient outcomes. As a company that purchases over a billion dollars of health care for its employees each year, the leadership of IBM also had a strong incentive to know what works with regard to care delivery.

"an immunization is due for our cat"

Toward that end Drs. Sepúlveda and Grundy began championing new models of patient-centered care, though not without the realization that there would be obstacles along the way.

"At the time, we recognized that this has all the features of a social movement," recalls Martin Sepúlveda, MD, FACP, IBM Fellow & VP, Healthcare Industries Research, who soon became a master strategist of fundamental health care reform in America.

So Dr. Sepúlveda pulled Dr. Paul Grundy in from his work in Singapore and together they orchestrated a social movement within the field of primary care medicine that was so far reaching in scope that it continues to this day.

"When I took the position at IBM," Dr. Grundy recalls, "I moved to New York. A few weeks after we got there we received a postcard in the mail. It was from our new veterinarian, reminding us that our cat is due for an immunization. My wife, however, never received any similar reminders about her mammography and other scheduled preventive measures."

This reminder of the state of preventive medicine and other experiences are formative for the new model of health care delivery that Drs. Sepúlveda and Grundy would help create.

Along the way, they are fortunate to look closely at some of the pioneering work being carried out at the University of Utah in the form of "Care by Design," one of the first models in the country to integrate acute, chronic and preventive care into a comprehensive delivery system. They examine the work of Kevin Grumbach, MD and Thomas Bodenheimer, MD at the University of California, San Francisco, with its strong focus on primary care and family and community medicine. They view the pioneering work carried out in the pediatrics field, and reviewed again Surgeon General Everett Koop's seminal

1987 report calling for coordinated, family-centered, community-based care for children with special health care needs and their families.

Drs. Sepúlveda and Grundy also familiarize themselves with the multi-dimensional Chronic Care Model that Edward Wagner had championed through his work at the University of Washington, Seattle. They study and they learn. They reach out for collaboration with others seeking the same goals. They observe and they listen carefully.

Around the same time back in Newport News, Dr. Anderson quietly begins putting some new procedures into place, the ones formed in the cauldron of his own practice, that would eventually become the *Family Team Care* model. He is building a prototype vehicle that will run on Dr. Sepúlveda's and Dr. Grundy's vision, and they are each working to fix at least some part of a broken health care system and rescue the primary care physician in the process.

A decade passes. We don't know how many thousands of hours Dr. Sepúlveda and Dr. Grundy and Dr. Anderson and other innovators have labored to re-design family physician care in America.

All we know is that they have done it. And they have done it just in time.

AMERICA'S CHAMPIONS OF PRIMARY CARE

"The establishment of the Patient-Centered Primary Care Collaborative institutionalized a movement. I honestly don't know if people understand how Dr. Grundy did this — or how do you go from that one idea to a Coalition with over 1,000 organizations."

— **Kavita Patel, MD**, Former director of policy for the White House Office of Public Engagement and Intergovernmental Affairs, previously deputy staff director for the Senate Health, Education, Labor and Pensions Committee under the leadership of the late Sen. Edward M. Kennedy. Dr. Patel is today a practicing internist and fellow and Managing Director of Delivery System Reform and Clinical Transformation at the Brooking Institution's Engelberg Center for Health Care Reform.

Peter Anderson, MD

CHAPTER 1

THE SKY IS FALLING
A Grand Experiment Begins

Everyone has a pain threshold. It's that often subtle distinction between merely sensing a stimulus and perceiving it to be painful. We all have a tolerance level, too, the point at which we can no longer endure the pain without physical or emotional damage.

Pain tolerance is sometimes explained through the every day example of placing your hand on a stove that's heating up and waiting until you can't hold it there any longer. Being the diverse lot that we are, some of us reach our tolerance level faster or more slowly than others. But eventually, every hand is going to move.

In my case, the hand pulled off the stove when both nurses in my office made the decision to quit. The fact is I had been feeling the heat rise for quite awhile. More on that a little later.

"when it was good"

I graduated from the University of Virginia Medical School in 1978. After a Family Medicine residency I begin practicing at a time when the future had a now unimaginable shine to it. There were challenges in getting a private practice underway, but they were expected and fairly easy to overcome. In a relatively short time my practice is successful.

Being a doctor and a primary care provider in particular is an important part of my mission in life. The work and the ability to make a difference in the lives of so many people is both humbling and gratifying. It also provides a means to help support my growing family.

While I accepted that this may not be *the* golden age of primary care, a time when a kindly Marcus Welby-type showed up on the doorstep with a black bag and a comforting smile, it was definitely *my* golden age. I have aspired to and become the *Familiar Physician*. Looking back on my practice, that's when it was good. And that's how it remained until we fast-forward about twenty years.

It's 2003 now and I am watching my medical practice become a burden financially, personally, professionally and on any other level you can think of. It's the same burden that so many other primary care physicians felt then and more are feeling now. That helpless sense that the sky is falling may be even worse in the present since today's version of health care reform can sometimes seem to be as much a part of the problem as a part of the solution.

At this point in my career I have been successful for two decades. I chose primary care so I could develop long-term relationships with my patients and for the most part, that's how it's worked out. My greatest professional satisfaction comes from being able to make a positive intervention, either in a treatment or preventive mode.

"the poster boy for the primary care crisis"

But by 2003 it's not working out so well anymore. For the first time in my professional life I am discouraged. That's on the better days. On the worse days I am demoralized by the realization that my best efforts are no longer enough to operate my practice on the highest possible level. When you look at measures like early retirement rates, satisfaction surveys and a lot of anecdotal evidence, it's clear that growing numbers of currently practicing primary care physicians (PCPs) are finding themselves in the same place.

At this point I feel like the poster boy for the primary care crisis that began kicking in hard around then and continues to this day. It's a crisis that we all need to be deeply concerned about and it affects everyone in America because all of us are connected to a health care system that simply isn't sustainable. And the fact that we can't maintain the status quo isn't entirely negative.

In a number of areas, technological achievements among them, Americans enjoy the best health care in the world. But the high level of quality and innovation doesn't extend across the board. For example, in a comparative study with 16 other developed nations in Europe, as well as Australia, Canada and Japan, the Institute of Medicine reports that Americans experience poorer overall health and die younger.

Similarly, a study by the National Institutes of Health identified "a pervasive pattern of shorter lives and poor health" when compared to other western democracies, despite the fact that the U.S. spends more on health care than those other countries. How much more? Estimates are that as a nation, we're spending about 17 percent of our gross domestic product, which comes out to be more than the next 10 big health care spending counties combined.

> *"you don't need a weather man to know which way the wind blows"*
> **— Bob Dylan**

There are a number of reasons why we're spending too much and not getting our money's worth in terms of better health outcomes. Our limited access to comprehensive primary care is considered to be one of the most significant.

To start with, the primary care pipeline isn't exactly gushing. Medical students may be busy, but they're not so busy to miss the fact that the Affordable Care Act (ACA) is going to bring a lot more people into the world of the insured and then straight into someone's medical office. That's good news in a well-running machine but a recipe for disaster in a dysfunctional system.

They also pick up quickly on the inequitable reality that starting salaries for primary care physicians are half or even a third of what other specialists or subspecialists can expect to make. Since the chance of coming out of medical school with some hefty debt is high, regardless of the specialty you're planning to pursue, earning potential can understandably tip the scale away from primary care.

One of numerous examples of the effect of this situation can be seen in a study by the Journal of the American Medical Association reporting that only 20 percent of internal medicine doctors — traditionally an important medical

"What is at the center of our system are the physicians, hospitals, pharmaceutical companies, and medical industry delivering the care, and the health insurance companies paying for it. This creates a mind-set of medicine as a business, a wealth-generating system, instead of medicine as a profession and a health-generating system. It creates confusion and complexity instead of clarity and simplicity."

—**Ted Epperly, MD**, Chairman, Center for Integration and Care Delivery of the Patient-Centered Primary Care Collaborative, Past President and Chairman, American Academy of Family Physicians, Author of *"Fractured: America's broken health care system and what we must do to heal it." (Sterling & Ross Publishers, 2012)* specialty reservoir for developing PCPs — are going into primary care medicine following their residency programs.

Combine these factors — not enough PCPs and not enough career appeal in the vision of an overworked and relatively underpaid doctor, with the still unknown pressures of health care reform — and it's clear that you're not going to require, to paraphrase Bob Dylan, the services of a meteorologist to determine the prevailing winds when it comes to primary care.

"…the next step before extinction"

The concerns I began to deal with in 2003 and the even more challenging situation we find ourselves in now have the potential, I would think the distinct likelihood, to negatively impact the profession of medicine, the field of primary care and the health of everyone in our country. So no matter who you are, if you think this problem doesn't affect you, think again.

As part of this bleak picture, I sometimes wonder if the primary care practitioner as we presently know him or her is going to become extinct. It would seem that there is too much at stake for that to happen and the provisions in the Affordable Care Act (ACA) designed specifically to improve the health of primary care should help incentivize the field.

At the same time, however, the ACA as it currently stands — and I can't overemphasize the sharpness of this two-edged sword — will add to the squeeze on primary care physicians who are already drowning in paperwork while being pummeled by a changing regulatory and reimbursement environment.

The reaction to this additional pressure, while it won't kill off primary care doctors directly, could help make the *Familiar Physician* approach to care — characterized by a strong and ongoing patient-physician bond and a level of comfort and trust that promotes the diagnostic and therapeutic processes — a thing of the past.

There's also a scenario envisioned by some people in which instead of leading the medical team in a re-structured patient encounter, the MD would be supplanted by non-physicians seeing patients in independent practices.

The alarm that I'm sounding here, and the reason I wrote this book, is that while primary care doctors won't succumb to a single catastrophic event like the theoretical asteroid impact that wiped out the dinosaurs, PCPs have

AMERICA'S CHAMPIONS OF PRIMARY CARE
"The idea, the vision and the leadership came from IBM's Martin Sepúlveda, MD, MPH, IBM Fellow & VP, Healthcare Industries Research."

—Dr. Paul Grundy

already become an endangered species. And for some creatures that's the next step before extinction.

"what can we learn from Massachusetts?"

When Massachusetts adopted its progressive health care law in 2006 with strong bipartisan support in the state government, a large percentage of its residents already had health insurance. Part of the legislation's intent, then, was to cover nearly everyone by plugging as many holes as possible in its system, short of evolving to a single payor option. I'm not suggesting that there is a direct correlation between the state and federal versions of health care legislation, nor am I making a judgment as to their relative merit.

What I would suggest, is that there are some correlations that may provide a glimpse of what we might expect when the insured patient pool is expanded.

So what can we learn from Massachusetts? According to the Huffington Post writer Steve LeBlanc, just half of primary care doctors in that state were taking new patients five years after the law went into effect, and average times for new patients seeking appointments with the doctors remained long — 45 days, up from 36 days the year before enactment — as reported through a Massachusetts Medical Society survey. Again, the situation may not be directly transferable to the ACA, but the specific situation regarding the influx of new patients isn't exactly promising.

So the core of the problem remains; if we as a nation are hoping to provide medical coverage for as many people as possible, we have to make sure that a sufficient number of doctors — as part of a larger, integrated system — are available to care for those people.

"never tell yourself it can't get any worse"

We're back to 2003 now and it's not good. My practice is losing $80,000 a year. Patients are calling with immediate concerns and we're telling them we can't see them today. I've tried all the conventional wisdom related to staffing ratios and scheduling procedures. But what's keeping me up nights, and I mean that literally, is the thought that we're coming too close to taking shortcuts.

When we have five or six patients backed up I worry that we're gathering only a portion, a large portion, but still a portion, of the information needed to make a solid medical evaluation. The need for gathering extensive amounts of data is especially critical with our growing numbers of older patients with chronic conditions.

When you add in the administrative and documentation requirements of the patient visit it's getting more and more difficult to fulfill my medical responsibility in the times allotted, which are back-to-back, daylong 15-minute encounters. Each day I ask myself if I'm being as thorough as possible in every case and each day the answer is creating more anxiety. The frustration that I'm feeling is shared by my patients who sense that at best, we're harried and that at worst, they're part of a medical practice assembly line.

Just as this feeling reaches its peak, my best nurses, Cathi Pope and Joyce Yates announce that they are considering quitting. They've been with me for 20 years and we've developed that kind of working relationship where just a look between us conveys pages of information.

Their rationale for leaving is summed up in their shared and obvious belief that they can get paid more to operate in misery and chaos somewhere else. (They were too kind to say this, but we all understood.) I've been aware that they've been looking at other opportunities for months and when they tell me their plans I can't even offer a counter argument let alone a counter offer. As painful as it is, I can't blame anyone for wanting to lower the lifeboats on a sinking ship.

It's one of those reminders to never tell yourself it can't get any worse.

"another rotten day"

When I get home later than I should — it's the time of that cold and rainy night you read about in the Prologue — dinner is a quiet and somewhat morose affair. With our children grown and out of the house, it's just my wife Laurie and me and I'm not holding up my end of the conversation very well.

"Another rotten day?" she asks, though by now it's pretty much of a rhetorical question. I tell her about Cathi and Joyce and their plans to leave the practice.

In what I look back on now as almost movie script timing, Laurie gets up from her chair, walks behind mine, and puts her arms around my neck, holding me silently for a long time.

"You used to love being a doctor," she said. "And it wasn't all that long ago."

"I know," I said, "but I don't love it anymore and I don't know how to make it better."

"I remember how energized and inspired you always were after coming back from a medical mission," she said. "You would tell me that along with the good work you and the team did it was also an adventure. That's what you called it, an adventure."

That was true, but I reminded her that this was not the best time to help provide medical care in developing and underserved parts of the world. At this point I might not have a practice to come back to.

"What I'm talking about" she said, "is the adventure part. You need something to take your mind off all of this. If it can be part of improving the situation in the office, so much the better. Like I said, you just have to think of it as going somewhere you haven't been before. Wherever that place is, it's got to be better than this."

Once again, it takes my best friend, my partner in love and life, the person who knows me better than anyone, to ignite the fire under me that I just couldn't seem to start.

"give me six months"

The next morning, I sit down with Cathi and Joyce. "Give me a little time," I said. "I'm ready to change the world."

I get a blank stare from both nurses and Joyce added that little head turn people do when they hear your words but aren't quite sure what you mean.

"OK," I said, "I'm exaggerating a bit about the whole world, but seriously, give me six months and together we'll change this practice. We'll redesign it. Better yet, we'll re-invent how we practice primary care here. If we can't make it work in that time, you're welcome to walk out the door and there's a very good chance I'll be leaving with you."

There is a silence, one of the longer ones I can remember ever having in a conversation and then without conferring together, they both say they'll talk it over with their families tonight and let me know in the morning.

Morning comes and they both agree to take part in the experiment.

AMERICA'S CHAMPIONS OF PRIMARY CARE

"We have had the answers for years in America, but we have been unwilling to change. I recently visited the head of health care for the nation of Spain, which has made great strides in re-engineering its medical system. I asked him how he got started. He said they hired an American consultant."

—Dr. Paul Grundy

CHAPTER 2

THE NEXT THOUSAND DAYS

Re-inventing the Exam Room

Before the thought of "a thousand days" makes you think the process of medical practice transformation requires more time than a space probe on its way to Saturn, let me clarify the chronology. When I told the nurses in my practice to give me six months, that's the amount of time I figured we would need to make changes in the exam room regarding the patient encounter and changing staff roles. That was what we were aiming for and as it turns out, we began experiencing the benefits of our redesign in as little as two months, and by six months or less everything in the exam room was running smoothly.

The thousand days — it was actually a little less, but nine hundred and something doesn't have the right sound to it — is what it took to really change the practice culture, develop the needed education and training, re-engineer our administrative infrastructure and build in performance measures. I would add that the importance of cultural change as the foundation for everything else shouldn't be underestimated.

Throughout the process we were careful to make sure that everyone involved, and that included input from patients, had a place at the table. At that time I was part of the non-profit Riverside Medical Group, one of Virginia's largest and most diverse multi-specialty groups, and the support provided by RMG leadership and all of my colleagues was invaluable.

"everything was taken away from me except practicing medicine"

For those first six months we have a special meeting every week for the sole purpose of re-creating our care delivery model. Diagnosis by diagnosis, we carefully detail the information we need to gather on the patient. We rehearse each step, over and over as if we're choreographing a theatrical production that we hope will have a very long run.

As it turns out, the choreography analogy is appropriate. Choreography doesn't just plan out the steps, patterns and sequences of movement in a dance or some other physical action, it symbolically records them in a way that they can be replicated by other "dancers." For that reason, we eventually put our new steps into a manual that we could refer to over time and that other practices could use as a guide.

While our efforts involved a considerable amount of detail the basic premise was that virtually everything was taken away from me except practicing medicine. Team efforts in general and nursing responsibilities in particular were subsequently increased.

"they were ready to burn the boats"

Initially the nurses were a little anxious about their changing roles and increased information-gathering duties. After some initial minor trepidation brought on by working at the top of their licenses, the nurses in my practice found the change to be both challenging and exhilarating. In a short time they were ready to burn the boats. There would be no going back to the way we did it before.

The result was a far greater level of satisfaction within the practice that translated almost immediately to our patients. In addition, we were able to get in virtually every patient who called with an urgent concern.

When I saw how effective the initial changes were I did something that would have been unimaginable when we started out on this course. I hired another medical assistant and a part-time registered nurse. The team is coming together and with a reduction in my non-clinical tasks, I am able to once again become that *Familiar Physician* for my patients. For the first time in years, maybe in the history of the practice, we have a true framework for moving forward.

As time passes we re-engineer those other aspects of the practice that affect patient care, but take place outside the exam room, everything ranging from scheduling and referrals to follow up, prescription refills and more.

"you're going to have some consequences downstream"

What I described in that transition to *inside the exam room* team care were the high points. There were low points, too. There were false starts and difficult days. There were also some doubts and a touch of confusion along the way and there was an ongoing recalculation of the time it would take.

Why? Because change is tough, particularly in a field that has a long tradition of being averse to change. People don't like to give up their traditional roles and I'm one of them. They don't like to do things differently because different doesn't always feel comfortable and who knows, it might even lead to mistakes. Beyond those cultural, personal and responsibility changes there are logistical challenges, too.

Moving away from the doctor-does-everything model when it relates to clinical care also requires technological upgrades and a considerable workflow revision. And of course, when you're dealing with workflow, just about every thing from a minor tweak to a major overhaul means you're going to have some consequence downstream along the lines of Newton's Third Law — for every action there is an equal and opposite reaction.

It's important for you to know that the process I'm looking back on was, in real time, accompanied by rigorous assessment, lengthy planning and considerable training prior to implementation. Once implemented the efforts to sustain the model are ongoing. Like they say, change isn't easy, but in this case the result was worth the work.

The story of *The Familiar Physician* is the story of the joy of practicing medicine.

A couple of years after our practice moved to the *Family Team Care* model, a 58-year-old adult male came in concerning a small lesion on his scalp. We will call him Bill.

Bill

This is how it usually happens. Bill is over 50 and has a skin problem. The doctor is rushed. Heart attacks kill more people than anything else in America, but the doctor is not going to ask Bill about his heart because Bill has come in for the skin lesion. The doctor does not have time for other issues, so no questions about Bill's heart are asked.

But in the *Family Team Care* model, the nurse had the time to ask some basic profile questions about chest pain, which under our new exam room process, are asked of every patient over 50. *Under the Family Team Care* model there is time to ask these preventive questions which were not related to the presenting symptoms.

Bill admitted that indeed he had been experiencing some discomfort when going up stairs.

We sent him to take a stress test, which resulted in the discovery of 80% blockage in four arteries. Bill received bypass surgery two days later and the nurse, because she had the time to ask, just may have saved the man's life.

That is what a *medical home* should do on a regular basis, using the *Family Team Care* model.

The physician is able to perform at the highest possible level and feels gratified knowing that his team has accomplished the goal of providing quality care for as many patients as possible.

Nurses now play a role that has been elevated to the top of their clinical license. *Inside the exam room Family Team Care* nurses have the confidence of knowing they are truly providing top-notch care.

"the team will see you now"

It's also important to know that what we accomplished was not the introduction of team-based care into medical practice. Working in a team is an essential element in the Chronic Care Model as well as with other clinical models throughout health care. Simply put, it has a history.

But here's how I would explain what we *did* do.

The first time that a team approach to care was used in the context of a medical practice would be hard if not impossible to establish. In fact, it's far more likely that it was a matter of evolution rather than revolution.

Let's assume, however, that there was a first time that the core process of "the doctor will see you now" was traded out for "the team will see you now." That first time, despite the incremental steps that undoubtedly preceded it would rightly be a breakthrough. It would be a true innovation for the practice that first put it into play.

"improving on the car, not the horse"

What we set out to do was to take that innovation and make it better. I believe that medicine, like most other fields, benefits greatly from this cycle of innovation and improvement because it all starts with an idea, but that idea has its greatest value when it can be executed. And successful execution is what we focused on.

I remember hearing a Henry Ford quote once in which he said if he had taken a poll and asked people what they really wanted during the time he was developing an affordable automobile, they probably would have said, "a faster horse."

In our case we were definitely improving on the car and not the horse. Practice transformation is that profound and for us there would be no return to the earlier approach. Staying with the analogy, our objective wasn't just to trade out an animal for a machine, but rather to make a car that was safer, drove better, used less fuel and provided a better overall experience for the drivers as well as the passengers.

SURVIVING THE TEMPEST

*The Perfect Storm bearing down
on primary care medicine*

Transitioning to *Team Care Medicine* occupied a lot of time and resources, all of which paid significant dividends to me, the staff, our families and our patients. What we had done, in addition to gaining greater financial stability and a vastly improved working environment, was to position ourselves to better meet the specific needs of our practice and the community we served.

But something larger was looming on the horizon that would sorely test — and will continue to challenge — our new approach to patient care. The clouds have been gathering for a decade or more but have begun to coalesce over the past few years. What I sense is that the changes we carried out in our practice were not only good business, but necessary for survival. Because a storm is on the way and the current and projected shortage of primary care physicians is only one of the forces at play.

**the perfect storm is the perfect metaphor
for the extraordinary circumstances we're facing**

The 1991 Perfect Storm, alternatively known as the Halloween Nor'easter of 1991 and popularized by a best selling book and subsequent

31

film, has since entered the language as a common descriptor of events or situations characterized by powerful converging forces.

The storm itself came into being when the remnants of Hurricane Grace collided with a low pressure system centered off Nova Scotia and a high pressure system that had moved up the spine of the Appalachians before taking a right turn toward Greenland. The storm caused severe coastal damage from winds and storm surge and created record high tides as well as rogue waves up to 100 feet high.

Tragically, the Perfect Storm also took the lives of 13 people including the six crewmen on the sword fishing boat, *Andrea Gail*, the subject of the book and film. For many, the visual of that boat's futile attempt to rise up and over a ten-story wave, featured on the cover of the book and the trailer of the movie, remains the symbol of this once-in-a-century meteorological phenomenon.

Despite the damage inflicted, however, the Perfect Storm was not a surprise. The Ocean Prediction Center, a component of the National Oceanic and Atmospheric Administration, and the National Weather Service both forecast a storm of epic proportions. As a result, warnings were issued to emergency service offices and the media well in advance. The advance warnings were then communicated to a skeptical public that for the most part took the forecast far too lightly.

This lack of concern, based in part on the particularly fine weather in evidence all along the New England and mid-Atlantic coasts at the time the alarm was sounded, proved to be a fatal error.

In fact, as the *Andrea Gail* motored out to its destiny, many coastal Massachusetts residents looked out over calm seas and fair skies while commenting on the uncharacteristically mild and sunny day they were enjoying in late October.

Some years after I read the *Perfect Storm* and later saw the movie, I began taking notes on several of the parallels between that event and what was going on in primary care. In a number of ways, the perfect storm is the perfect metaphor for the extraordinary circumstances we are facing. Among the more direct comparisons are the multiple forces coming together at the same or close to the same time as well as the lack of concern (an attitude not universal, but common) among both the medical profession and the general public. Like the storm warnings, many of us are aware but skeptical.

In both cases, it would appear that people just can't imagine they'll ever have to get to the top of that 100-foot wave before it crests.

If there is a marked difference between the literal perfect storm and the figurative one, it is a matter of degree. While the weather event was the result of three major systems, the storm already darkening the skies over primary care medicine is coming from at least nine major forces.

Nine Storms Converging on Primary Care:
Storm #1
The Patient Protection and Affordable Care Act

The Affordable Care Act (ACA) has not created the primary care crisis on its own. However, it will help reveal the fractures in the current system and contribute to the pressures already directed to the PCP unless we effectively re-engineer the way we care for patients.

"...could be the beginning of a brilliant new age of primary care, or an accelerant to the dawn of the fall of primary care"

While the jury is still out on exactly when it will happen, we can expect a large number of newly insured patients — estimates range between 30 and 40 million people —- will be presenting themselves to primary care doctors. As waiting rooms fill up, many doctors will not be in a position to take new patients. At the same time, as a counter force, reduced reimbursements may force (in the always questionable economic model of "make it up in volume") many doctors to see more patients in order to keep their practices viable.

**"somewhere in that we lose the humanity...
the system begins to chew them up"**

My colleague, Dr. Paul Grundy, is frank about the broken payment system in America and its affect on the people it's meant to serve. "The rewards system in health care is so convoluted that people become opportunities to make money. Somewhere in that we lose the humanity. The system begins to chew them up."

"imagine...every time you're sick, you're a stranger, enduring long waits for someone to help solve your problem that has likely never seen you before"

Regardless of your personal stand on health care reform (and I personally have found myself on both sides of the legislation depending on specific issues) the fact is that on June 28, 2012, the United States Supreme Court upheld the constitutionality of most of the reform act in the case National Federation of Independent Business v. Sebelius.

Based on conversations with colleagues and friends I am not alone in my contention that the success of this legislation in particular and health care delivery in general depend a great deal on a robust primary care workforce.

I believe further that this reform will be at its most effective if it helps strengthen the *doctor-patient relationship* as a powerful, quality-producing, cost effective concept in medicine.

In casual conversations as well as major presentations I ask people to "imagine health care without the *Familiar Physician*."

"Every time you're sick, you're a stranger, enduring long waits for someone to help solve your problem … someone who may have never seen you before."

As I mentioned early, the Massachusetts experience, probably the closest model we have to compare with the ACA, reveals that only half of the primary care doctors in that state are able to accept new patients.

In the year's time between 2010 and 2011, the number of insured Americans on a national scale grew by just 3.6 million people, an increase of less than 1.5 percent. The instantaneous 15 percent increase in the number of insured Americans will undoubtedly shock the system, which is accustomed to a much slower growth. The potential for serious gridlock is clear.

So what we're left with is somewhat of a paradox. The ACA, which should be a positive force in improving access to coverage and, ultimately, to care, also carries within it the potential to crush primary care.

Nine Storms Converging on Primary Care:
Storm #2
Baby Boomers Surging into Physician Offices

Every day in America 10,000 people turn 65. One way to look at those numbers is to consider that in just one month's time it's as if a city the size of Toledo suddenly appears with every resident ready to access Medicare. This month, next month, every month.

Continuing with the social math, add another week or so and you've got a Pittsburgh full of these aging Baby Boomers. In just four months at the current rate of newly minted 65 year olds, you're looking at a population as big as Dallas all of whom find themselves suddenly comparing notes on Medicare Part B.

You get the picture. There are quite a few older adults coming down the road. And in most cases it's a road leading right to the primary care office where they're going to be playing musical chairs with all those newly insured people.

"Baby Boomers," and I count myself in their number, are people born between 1946 and 1964. Various studies over the years have shown that the majority of Baby Boomers (estimates range up to 70%) have at least one chronic illness, and may have up to five as they continue to age. In our practice we have already experienced lengthier and more complicated visits with our aging patients.

Managing multiple chronic illnesses takes time and can be expensive. The problem is that on average, physicians earn 20% to 30% less from Medicare than they do from private patients. As a result, many doctors are dropping out of the program. In the area of primary care, a traditional bulwark of care for older adults, it's estimated that around 90% of physicians participate in Medicare. A smaller percentage, however, are accepting new patients so the trend is not good, and it's likely to get worse.

"the dramatic increase in older Americans
is already here and growing fast"

Along with all those new 65-year-olds, there are quite a few older Americans around. In fact, the 85 and over age group is one of the fastest growing among the general population. In 1996 there were about 4 million people in the U.S. over 85 years old. In just four years the number increased to 6.7 million adults over 85 with the projection that by 2040 there will be 13 million.

This trajectory in of itself is not catastrophic since the rise will be relatively gradual and steady. What may add severe stress to the system, however, are the breakthroughs predicted in genomic science and regenerative medicine that are expected to make significant inroads against cancer, diabetes, heart disease and stroke within the next several decades.

What tempers the good news about increased life expectancy is that we can only hope that other older adult afflictions, including Alzheimer's disease, which is predicted to double by midcentury, will also be reduced through research breakthroughs and biomedical and technological innovation.

Whatever the future holds in this area, the one thing we can be virtually certain about is that there will be more aging Americans, more chronic conditions, and possibly, fewer (and more stressed) primary care physicians.

Nine Storms Converging on Primary Care:
Storm #3
Longer Workdays, Reduced Reimbursement, Failing Practices

The looming possibility of financial failure changes everything.

Primary care physicians across America are struggling to make the business end of their practice work. Many of them have already lost the ability to fully enjoy their personal lives and families, take vacations and carry out a normal workday schedule.

Office staffs are harried and swamped with electronic medical records, insurance forms, referrals, appointments, daily urgent call-ins, scheduling testing, reporting results, answering the telephone, patient care and comfort and little time to take a deep breath.

"the chaos of uncertainty haunts
the primary care practice environment"

The cuts to physician payments are a steady sound from Washington and the chaos of uncertainty haunts the primary care practice environment.

It is particularly difficult for physicians to continue seeing a growing rise in Medicare beneficiaries, especially in small or solo practices, with the constant threat of Medicare payments being cut by 25% or more.

This difficulty coincides with a time in which as a nation, we are leaning hard on this group of primary care doctors to guide us through the new health care landscape. In a dysfunctional payment system based on volume rather than value, many primary care practices have neither the incentive nor the time to follow up on patients they way they would like to or to provide more comprehensive medical management.

Resources for management and overall coordination are especially strained when older patients are seen by several different specialists.

I worry about the patients.

Nine Storms Converging on Primary Care:
Storm #4
The Pharmaceutical Revolution

The role of innovative drug treatments throughout the history of medicine, and especially the pharmaceutical revolution of the past several decades, is monumental. The result has been a remarkable record of improved health outcomes and quality of life, what some have considered a man-made miracle.

At the same time, however, the prescription drug expenditures are among the most rapidly growing components among total health care expenditures. In fairness, a large part of the expenditures are related to increased utilization. But costs are increasing.

The result of these increases, coupled with higher co-pays and other forms of increased cost sharing on the part of patients, is associated with decreased adherence to treatment regimens and even the discontinuation of needed medications.

To put a human face on it, as a physician, I am all too keenly aware that substantial numbers of patients without solid financial resources, along with older adults on fixed incomes, are prone to break pills in half or take them every other day. Cost isn't the only reason that an estimated one out of two patients don't take their medications exactly as prescribed, but it's up there.

For the primary care physician, poor compliance with medications (or adverse reactions even when compliance is perfect) often means an additional visit or multiple visits to her or his office, often accompanied by a reduced Medicare reimbursement. So for that already overburdened practitioner the cycle continues.

Other areas related to the pharmaceutical revolution impact the physician's time, which in turn, is linked to his or her ability to provide quality patient care. For example, the amount of medical management related solely to medications has increased in direct proportion to the number of prescriptions held by the patient. Over the course of my practice, those numbers have increased significantly.

"...an average of roughly 13 prescriptions for each man, woman, and child"

A recent article in Medical News Today estimates that the number of prescriptions for drugs written each year in America comes out to the nice round number of four billion.

That's an average of roughly 13 prescriptions for each man, woman, and child — about one new prescription every month for every American.

Digging a little deeper, the administration of prescriptions goes far beyond the act of simply writing the script and handing it to a patient. A systematic approach advocated by the World Health Organization illustrates just how detailed and complicated the process has become. Their eight-step approach checklist includes:

- evaluate and clearly define the patient's problem
- specify the therapeutic objective
- select the appropriate drug therapy
- initiate therapy with appropriate details and consider non-pharmacologic therapies
- give information, instructions, and warnings
- evaluate therapy regularly (e.g., monitor treatment results, consider discontinuation of the drug)
- consider drug cost when prescribing
- use an electronic medical record or other computer-based tools to reduce prescribing errors

Using electronic medical record prescribing software and having access to drug references electronically, given the proliferation of new drugs, is now essential rather than optional. In fact, keeping up on the expanding literature associated with these new pharmaceuticals is basically a new and separate skill set.

The pharmaceutical revolution has unequivocally benefited drug companies and with only minor exception has benefited everyone in America by providing some of our greatest medical innovations with regard to better health over longer lifetimes. On both a personal and professional level, I am grateful for the vision, the research, the laborious translation from lab bench to bedside and the commitment that has made these breakthroughs possible over the years.

As a primary care physician, however, I would also say that, based on the reasons I mentioned with regard to compliance and management time, the rapid and continuing expansion of pharmaceutical options represents still another of the converging storms washing over primary care medicine.

Nine Storms Converging on Primary Care:
Storm #5
Pessimism Numbs Innovation

The Physicians Foundation, a non-profit organization that "seeks to advance the work of the practicing physician" recently conducted one of the largest and most comprehensive physician surveys ever carried out. The survey reached over 630,000 doctors (almost 85% of all physicians actively engaged in patient care) selected from the nation's largest physician database.

The study was developed to reveal, among other areas of clinician response, current morale levels, perspectives on health care reform, practice patterns, career plans and issues impacting patient care.

The study indicated that the malaise I have personally experienced along with a number of my physician colleagues in primary care and other specialties was impacting many other doctors within the profession.

"over 60 percent of physicians
would retire today if they could"

Over three quarters of the doctors surveyed revealed themselves to be somewhat or very pessimistic about the future of the medical profession, and over 80 percent agree it's in decline. Keep in mind this included physicians at all stages in their careers, not just older doctors looking back on "the good old days" and bemoaning the loss.

A distinct majority would not recommend medicine as a career. Over a third would not personally choose medicine again for their own career. Over 60 percent of physicians would retire today if they could.

While uninsured patients, at least those who can follow along with the reams of description that are part of the ACA, may be applauding what on paper will be improved access, the physician community is far less optimistic.

Physicians know only too well that the improved access in general and optimal outcomes in particular will be complicated for many people by the fact that they haven't had a regular doctor for years. In the past, many of these individuals countered a lack of health insurance by going to emergency rooms for care, paying cash or nothing at all and ignoring all but the direst of symptoms. Now, they may be postponing any type of treatment in anticipation of finally being covered. As a result, medical problems will be more complex and expensive.

The high probability of a far heavier patient load (and its implications for a physician's quality of life) combined with a higher percentage of complex medical needs is another brick in the wall of discouragement.

For many practitioners the surge of more and sicker patients threatens to overwhelm an already fragile practice within a damaged and disillusioned primary medicine community. At the same time it drains the time, energy and creativity that could otherwise be directed toward care delivery innovation.

The inability to find solutions, brought on by the sheer weight and number of the problems is part of the reality that led so many current doctors in the Physicians Foundation survey to express their strong pessimism. And it's what's influencing growing numbers of medical students and residents to vote with their feet when it comes to choosing a career in primary care.

Nine Storms Converging on Primary Care:
Storm #6
Not Enough Young Physicians Are Choosing Primary Care

Even before the full tsunami of older adults and newly covered people of all ages reaches our medical offices, clinics and hospitals, it should be clearly noted that the United States is already behind in the number of primary care doctors needed to care appropriately for our population.

Government studies indicate that underserved areas in the U.S. (and these range from rural to urban) currently need 16,679 more primary care physicians to reach a "medically appropriate" target of 1 for every 2,000 residents.

The number of primary care physicians needed now is projected to rise to 50,000 by 2025. Going back once again to the Massachusetts model of health reform we can understand at least part of the problem.

According to Alan H. Goroll, MD, a professor of medicine at Harvard Medical School and a practicing PCP, the Massachusetts health care initiative is an example of what can go wrong if the primary care system isn't fixed simultaneously with the start of expanded coverage.

As a brief reminder, Massachusetts passed legislation in 2006 that has helped increase the percentage of insured residents to 97.4 percent of its population, the highest in the U.S.

Dr. Goroll's cautionary tale, delivered in September of 2010, reveals that the average waiting time for a considerable number of these insured individuals to see a primary care doctor in Boston, a city with 14 teaching hospitals, is 63 days, the most among 15 cities in a 2009 survey by Merritt Hawkins & Associates, a national recruiting and research firm.

So we are already short and the pipeline isn't looking promising.

In the late 1990's and early 2000's, I no longer encouraged medical students to go into primary care, something I had done in my previous years as a PCP. That period represented some of the worst years of primary care and no relief was in sight from the increased paperwork, rushed visits, dissatisfied patients, reimbursement disparities and the need to bring work home that I was personally experiencing.

It's true that I may have reached a very few individuals with my dire forecast but the impetus for the decline was moving forward on a far larger scale.

Medical students and residents who are shunning primary care can readily discern that large numbers of physicians have little optimism that the system in general and primary care in particular will be fixed easily or soon. What they see instead are high numbers of PCPs who have retired early or changed careers and what they hear are serious laments on the disappearance or at least the considerable curtailment of the enjoyment and gratification that men and women once found in primary care.

What they also are aware of is a primary care system that has failed, as Cuba Gooding Jr. famously put it to Tom Cruise in the movie, *Jerry Maguire*, to "Show me the money."

"today, family doctors make about one half of the income of other medical specialties"

Dr. Goroll's presentation expressed the feelings of many of us in primary care medicine when he addressed the payment issue before some of the nation's top health care leaders.

"We in the primary care community have been uncomfortable talking about payment. It's not what drove us into the practice of medicine and talking about it always felt self-serving."

But if it isn't what drove existing PCPs into medicine, it is managing to drive prospective ones away.

By the time their years of training is concluded, these recently minted doctors, assuming they traveled the traditional college to med school to residency route are about 30 years old and in need of a stable financial present as well as future. Given that the typical medical student debt is about $140,000, the income disparities prove to be "strong disincentives for younger physicians," according to a 2009 report from the American College of Physicians.

Although it can vary somewhat, many family doctors today make about one half of the income of other medical specialties. Over the course of a long career it's been estimated that the compensation gap can add up to over $3 million dollars.

Recognition of the payment differential can be seen in a 2008 survey of third-year medical residents conducted by the American College of Physicians in which 21 percent said they planned to pursue careers in general internal medicine, the equivalent of primary care. Only ten years earlier, the figure was 54 percent.

Some of my colleagues who entered medicine about the same time I did believe that the decline in the PCP training ranks is related to a parallel decline in personal commitment or altruism. I don't agree with that assessment. I think today's generation of college pre-med students, medical students and residents is rich in idealism and continues to hold the basic belief that the medical profession offers a rare chance to make a difference.

At the same time, they are realists. They look around at the primary care field and see uncertainty and discontent. They see also that their very hard work and the significant debt that generally goes with it will lead them to the bottom of the pay scale within their profession. I think the majority of students respect primary care and understand that it's the backbone of the U.S. health care system. I think they admire primary care physicians.

But for some clearly defined reasons, they don't want to be one.

And the mismatch of supply and demand couldn't have come at a worse time. As Beverly Woo, MD, of Brigham and Women's Hospital in Boston so powerfully stated the problem, "Although the line of students signing up for a career in primary care medicine is getting shorter, the line of patients in need of primary care doctors is getting longer every day."

Nine Storms Converging on Primary Care:
Storm #7
Ever-Present Malpractice Threat

In the extensive study conducted by the Physicians Foundation that I mentioned earlier, *A Survey of America's Physicians: Practice Patterns and Perspectives*, some interesting information came to light when physicians were asked about the least satisfying part of their medical practice. The survey identified "liability and defensive medicine" as the prime nemesis, followed by "Medicare, Medicaid and other government regulations; payment issues; and uncertainty about changes occurring as a result of health care reform."

So doctors are concerned — and other words like "resentful" and "angry" often come into play — not only at the threat of being sued, but also the corresponding need to practice expensive defensive medicine, not in order to validate a diagnosis, but to reduce the risk of a lawsuit.

The threat of a malpractice suit has also been part of the seeming necessity of operating in a large medical group, often as an employee, as a strength in numbers strategy rather than opting for a sole or smaller private practice.

And meanwhile, along with the threat of litigation and the defensive medical practices intended to reduce it, the message of cost reduction via fewer expensive diagnostic tests becomes louder and louder.

While there is considerable variation involving malpractice on a state-by-state basis, the national picture reveals that the total number of lawsuits is on a downward trajectory. This direction is balanced, however, by the fact that the actual amounts per damage awards — awards in medical malpractice dwarf those in other injury-related cases — are growing. And in a perfect storm within a perfect storm, this development is taking place at a time when premiums are rising again after a recent plateau while the number of firms offering coverage decreases.

To round out the picture, the problem is widely distributed. A 2010 American Medical Association Physician Practice Information survey reveals that nearly 40% of primary care physicians have been sued in their careers, as have 34% of general internists. As you might expect, the numbers get even higher for surgeons.

In addition to the costs of malpractice insurance, the long hours involved in dealing with lawsuits can represent a considerable drain on time. In many cases, claims, even those not leading to lawsuits, can take years to resolve.

According to the Physician Insurers Association of America (PIAA), a group of doctor-owned or operated liability carriers, the highest percentage of malpractice suits, more than one third, are related to errors in diagnosis.

These claims are often complicated by insufficient documentation on the chart, and poor communication between physician and patient, both of which can be attributable to the inefficient business model and structure currently in place in many medical offices in America.

Within this context, the one thing that does look fairly certain based on both research and a very large amount of anecdotal evidence is the relationship between medical malpractice filings and the erosion of the interpersonal relationship between doctor and patient. The slow but steady disappearance of *The Familiar Physician* is creating a lack of trust, a weakening of the traditional bond between provider and consumer that even state tort reform and improved risk management won't improve.

Nine Storms Converging on Primary Care: Storm #8
The Coming Wave of Physician Retirements

It's been estimated that one out of three practicing physicians in the United States is over the age of 55. As a result, a significant percentage of doctors are approaching full retirement age and many of them can't wait.

In addition, a high percentage of physicians are facing burnout and are ready to retire early. As we have seen, surveys show that over sixty percent say they would retire early, if they could afford to do so.

With the older adult population growing, the demand for physicians will intensify over the coming years. According to American Association of Medical Colleges estimates, the United States faces a shortage of more than 90,000 physicians (of all specialties) by 2020 — a number that will grow to more than 130,000 by 2025.

"I can understand the powerlessness many seasoned doctors feel"

The surveys indicate that as many as 60 percent of physicians over the age of 55 will retire in the next three years. The more seasoned physicians, who have already endured the transition to electronic medical records, the advent of HMO's, bundled payments, being acquired by a larger group practice, have too many battle scars to face another round of major change.

With my kids up and grown and off on their own, I have asked myself the retirement question regularly over the last ten years. So I can understand the sense of powerlessness many seasoned doctors feel. At this point, I don't know too many colleagues who if they haven't set a retirement date in stone, have at least penciled it in on the calendar.

Nine Storms Converging on Primary Care:
Storm #9
Electronic Medical Record Stress

First of all, I want to be totally clear that I am a strong advocate of the electronic medical record and recognize its potential to improve the quality, safety and efficiency of care while adding to patient empowerment. Patients have too many data points — sometimes as many as 300 — for paper charts to be competent. A well-implemented EMR also provides a significant administrative benefit for the practice through its improved accuracy including the ability to reduce billing re-codes and re-submissions. I would also add that while the data entry part of the EMR process can feel a little clunky at times for anyone who grew up on paper charts, you can't beat the ease of retrieval and sharing.

Having said that, I now want to mention that if you're a physician who hasn't already made the transition, it will take longer to implement and cost more than you imagined or planned. And the learning curve may be steeper than you think, especially when it comes to customizing the EMR for a specific medical practice.

Putting it into very simple terms, what the EMR represents for a large portion of primary care physicians, especially those not employed by a health care organization, is both a blessing and a curse.

> "after ten years of medical training, I was staring
> down at a computer with a patient in the room"

As part of a large multi-specialty group practice that pioneered the EMR in its region, my personal experience was that of an early adopter. While that brought a certain sense of satisfaction, I have to admit that my first thought after I actually began using the EMR was wondering how I came to the point where, after ten years of medical training, I was staring down at a computer instead of looking at the patient in the room. Despite a bit of initial disorientation and the expected glitches, I was quick to see the benefits. At the same time I was aware that the cost, which included acquiring the technology and the hardware along with the ongoing IT support, was a high hurdle for many practices to get over. And as part of the learning curve, this new tool, which was supposed to help me become more efficient, had cut my daily productivity by 35%!

Now, physicians transitioning from paper offices to electronic ones who can meet the "meaningful use" criteria can take advantage of the Medicare and Medicaid incentive programs established through the Recovery Act/ HITECH Act of 2009. But the costs you may not consider involve a substantial disruption of workflow in areas like billing and accounts receivable, basic patient documentation, scheduling, lab results, sharing patient information and more. Along with that workflow disruption (and it will never move ahead faster than the weakest link in your collective learning curve chain) there's a large chunk of time given up for initial as well as ongoing training.

Considering that many primary care doctors are already harried and working close to the margin, the time demands of adopting the EMR can feel crushing. I don't know any physicians who are pushing back on doing the electronic medical record. But I don't know too many who haven't yet converted who are not dreading the process or who are struggling to maintain sanity while they do it.

This is undoubtedly related to my own experience, but my sense is that conversions to EMR systems represent one of the most stressful moments in a physician's career. Again, it's one of those mini-convergences within the larger perfect storm — the physician and entire office staff are learning not just a new way of documentation, but a new approach to patient care, and all the while the never-ending line of patients is still coming into the office.

And it's a tough ride for doctors in a large medical group as well as those on their own. For the group-based physicians the EMR has likely been pressed down from above, and many doctors, present company included, don't enjoy being managed excessively. To up the degree of difficulty, some of the EMR systems are not as user friendly as they could be and have been rushed to implementation by the federal government's adoption incentives. So at least for a while, and it can feel like quite a while, the EMR is disrupting a lot more than it is facilitating.

For independent practitioners, still the nation's largest percentage of primary care physicians (and least able to bear the loss of productivity), there is sticker shock at the cost of an effective EMR system in an environment of reimbursement cutbacks. This one issue, more than any other single factor, has been the prime motivator for pushing otherwise unwilling doctors into large medical groups.

The truth is, no one doubts that this particular storm pattern has a lot of blue sky and fair weather behind it. Nonetheless, it initially hits like a Force 12 on the Beaufort scale.

CHAPTER 3

HOPE ON THE NATIONAL HORIZON

Here Comes IBM

Meanwhile, about 430 miles to the north of my office, at IBM World Headquarters, Dr. Martin Sepúlveda formulates a strategy to transform American medicine.

His study of the broken U.S. health care system is complete. He knows that nothing short of completely re-designing the foundation of American health care will work.

The awakening of a nation would be done one stakeholder at a time.

a master strategist begins his plan
Dr. Martin Sepúlveda

"If we view this from 5,000 feet, there are critical points in the historical timeline from an IBM perspective," he recalls.

"First, I meet with forty different companies and bring the business community into the planning. We unite the buyers of health care."

Dr. Sepúlveda recalls the essence of the early conversations with the "House of Primary Care."

"Next, a few months later, Dr. Grundy and I meet with the four primary care medical associations."

"Drs. Martin Sepúlveda and Paul Grundy of IBM developed a strategy not to come up with the full shape of health care reform — only one vital piece.

They came up with a platform that would enable good medicine to thrive. Just the platform. Then they began to champion that idea.

The ***medical home.*** It's here. Or coming."

"Here's what we would like to do," he told them.

"And it can't be done without your help."

"We are health care buyers. You are health care providers. You have the right vision, but as a bridge between the corporate world and the world of medicine I think we can help you take that vision to an entirely different level and as such, I offer you a proposition."

"One — Come together, develop an integrated uniform proposal. Dr. Paul Grundy will help you achieve this. This will be a business proposition. Policymakers will listen. Business is demanding it now. We will help you in any way possible."

The "House of Primary Care"

American Academy of Pediatrics
Founded 1930
60,000 primary care and subspecialty doctors

American Academy of Family Physicians
Founded 1947
100,000 primary care doctors

American Osteopathic Association
Founded 1897
78,000 osteopathic medical doctors

American College of Physicians
Founded 1915
133,000 primary care and subspecialty physicians

"Two — Sit in the trenches with business people who can sometimes be bare-knuckle and in-your-face, expecting you to be accountable in the way they view accountability. I would be glad to offer any insights I might have on how to talk with them and think like them, as a way toward understanding their perspective now."

"Three — We are going to form an organization where payors (insurance companies are not really payors) create a vehicle for how to accomplish the needed changes. We will recruit other players into this organization."

After presenting this proposal, Dr. Sepúlveda picks his team, first bringing in Paul Grundy, MD who was, at that time, working at the intersection of health and diplomacy in Singapore. Then Christopher Nohrden, a long time IBM employee joins the team to offer his expertise in health information technology and logistics. As a former nurse, paramedic and Vietnam-era Navy Corpsman, Chris was another strong link between the corporate world and hands-on health care.

Drs. Sepúlveda and Grundy know that no matter what shape reform would take in the coming years, if they could help assure a strong base of primary care, a *"Familiar Physician"* for most Americans, whatever came to be built on that foundation would result in a better health care experience for everyone, including those employers who are a big part of paying the bills.

"…they did it in relative public silence
until their vision of a *medical home* for every American
is embedded in the new health care reform law"

They do their homework. They find a potential solution to one of the core problems in this nation's medical system. Then they gather health care stakeholders around them and in the process, unite the field of health care — at the very least a good portion of it — like few other endeavors.

As they formulate the campaign, my Newport News-based practice is nearing a breakthrough moment.

Our grand experiment is clearly working. Our revenue is going up more than $100,000 per year. More importantly, we experience a dramatic improvement in our quality measures. We received the NCQA national heart/stroke recognition for quality.

In addition, our patient satisfaction goes way up, the staff is really enjoying their work, and my workweek dropped to 45 or 50 hours per week —and I could finally have unpressured time with my family again.

AMERICA'S CHAMPIONS OF PRIMARY CARE

"When Paul reached out to all the constituents in the field, he reached out with the organizational model America's pediatricians had brought forth forty years ago — the basic *medical home* model."

—**Christopher Nohrden**, IBM retiree, and former Director of eLearning for the *PCPCC*.

Once the team was built and trained, or more appropriately, rebuilt and re-trained in what we now call *Family Team Care*, I find that it's easy to deliver primary care in a way that I have always known is the "right way."

Same-day access to a *Familiar Physician*, timely communications, competent care for acute and chronic needs, quality improvement and population management are well known goals to anyone with a primary care medical education, but not easily obtained.

Now with the adequate staff and the productivity to pay for the staff under normal and customary fee schedules, I am able to meet patient needs.

"...many colleagues around me are still struggling"

On the most basic terms I have reclaimed the joy and pleasure of medicine. Yet, I feel as if I am an exception. Many colleagues around me are still struggling. Around this time I begin to have the sense that my calling as a physician includes helping them, too.

"...a glimmer of hope"

And at that very moment — a glimmer of hope for the field of primary care, which is still preparing to be crushed by the perfect storm, appears on the horizon.

While we are on our journey of re-inventing primary care delivery and creating an innovative new model within a single medical office, Dr. Sepúlveda taps Dr. Grundy to become a major leader and spokesperson for quality primary care medicine in America, we start hearing about this internationally recognized physician who is starting to champion primary care on a very large stage.

Dr. Paul Grundy notices that a little inspiration may be in order.

"We can fix this," he gently says.

Having the lofty title of Director of Healthcare Transformation for IBM, he and Dr. Sepúlveda now have over a half million insured lives in their hands.

Dr. Grundy fine-tunes his message around the country. In 2006, IBM provides over $1.7 billion a year in health benefits to employees, and he leads a corporate juggernaut that is not happy with the wasteful, broken health care system.

After a thorough study, IBM recognizes that nothing less than the renaissance of primary care is needed. At the heart of their effort to revive primary care, Dr. Grundy gathers his strength.

"Paul can capture the hearts of people," notes Dr. Sepúlveda.

And part of the reason his message is so powerful is that it represents a very large number of people.

I am soon to meet him.

the promise of the *medical home*

I am in one of the many audiences that Dr. Grundy is addressing across the country at this time. He speaks about the role that large corporations like IBM play as buyers of health care and how they are affected by inefficiencies in the system. During his talk and then later when I meet him he continues to champion primary care as an essential component in meaningful health care reform. He talks about the promise of the *medical home.*

Hearing Dr. Grundy champion primary care reinforces the idea that now that I have found a more effective way to practice primary care I should share it.

"…primary care will become intolerable without major change"

I realize even more that if we don't bring back the pleasure and personal gratification of practicing medicine to the field, nothing that is being engineered at the national level will work. And as part of a continuous feedback loop, without major change there won't be much pleasure to go around.

Dr. Grundy believes in sharing, too, though he is carrying it out on a much larger scale. Dr. Grundy has seen the vital importance of a robust primary care system in other developed nations. He has an idea about what works and he's attuned to the differences in the political and cultural systems that are part of making it work.

As one of their first steps once they've put a team together, Drs. Sepúlveda and Grundy draw dozens of colleagues from other Fortune 100 self-insured corporations together, along with representatives from throughout the U.S. health care world.

AMERICA'S CHAMPIONS OF PRIMARY CARE

"IBM's Martin Sepúlveda, MD, MPH, said part of his job as vice president of global well-being services and global health benefits, is to develop policies and strategies to keep IBM employees as fit, productive and innovative as they can be.

'We have a stake in addressing those root causes of the dysfunction in our health care system, and one of the most neglected and glaring root causes of that dysfunction is the crisis in the decline of primary care,' he said' ."

— **Sheri Porter**, Associate Editor,
AAFP News Now, November 2008

"voice of change"

Here, they form a voice of change that cannot be ignored. Some of the largest private buyers of health care in the U.S. and the world have drawn the line. Insurance companies are quick to notice.

The coalition is formed to support a simple but powerful idea — laying down the Patient-Centered Medical Home model beneath everything in primary care medicine specifically in order to reach health care in general.

Quickly, he discovers that this message has resonance beyond the international corporate world. An awkward reunion is planned. Awkward because health care providers from a wide range of professional and personal backgrounds are gathering together to support a big idea. This has never happened in America before on such a scale.

When we remember our look at the convergence of forces hitting primary care doctors, it's easy to understand how the first thing we need to offer them is hope.

Toward that end, the way in which Dr. Grundy helped bring together disparate and rarely aligned partners finally opened a door, only slightly at first, but enough to allow in a crack of light, in the very dark room where many family doctors had been dwelling.

"...an important part of primary care medicine in America depends on these two visionaries being successful"

I recount the story of Drs. Sepúlveda and Grundy's work at IBM because an important part of primary care medicine in America depends on these two visionaries being successful in their effort to unite people around a common goal.

And what they work toward is more and more taking the form of the *medical home*.

The Patient-Centered Medical Home concept of care was introduced by the American Academy of Pediatrics Council on Pediatric Practice in 1967 and later adopted in 2002 by the primary care specialty as part of its "Future of Family Medicine" project.

But it is Dr. Martin Sepúlveda and Dr. Paul Grundy and the power of the coalition led by IBM that offers up the *medical home* model as the future of health care in America. They begin to make a powerful argument.

the idea and the vision: Dr. Martin Sepúlveda

"The idea, the vision and the leadership came from IBM's Martin Sepúlveda, MD, MPH, IBM Fellow & VP, Healthcare Industries Research," notes Dr. Paul Grundy.

"…change the covenant"

Dr. Sepúlveda made a major presentation to the American Academy of Family Physicians Board in May 2006, in which he positioned a solid primary care foundation as the most effective strategy for moving forward. He outlined why IBM thought it was so important to strengthen primary care and the very clear rationale of why they were willing to help. In that year alone, IBM would spend $1.7 billion on making sure 540,000 people worldwide had access to health care.

Dr. Paul Grundy recalls a pivotal meeting.

"In fact, the very first engagement and what opened my eyes was at an informal meeting Martin held at his home in 2006."

J. Randall MacDonald

Dr. Grundy paints the picture of a gathering with top executives Dr. Sepúlveda, and J. Randall MacDonald as the seminal moment when IBM assumed the role of champion of primary care. Randy MacDonald joined IBM in 2000 as Senior Vice President, Human Resources, responsible for the global human resources practices, policies and operations of the organization.

"This meeting epitomized the very best of Randy MacDonald, who recently retired from IBM following a distinguished career. Randy's unique gift is a clear, laser-like vision about right and wrong, and a will to do something about it. The conversation that day centered around just that, what is right and wrong with health care in America."

"We began by asking ourselves one primary question: 'How do we change the covenant between the buyer of care and the provider of care to get at a better value proposition?' "

creating the Collaborative

One way was for IBM to work more directly with the providers to create the Patient-Centered Primary Care Collaborative (PCPCC), a group of large employers and the major primary care physician associations: American Osteopathic Association (AOA), American Academy of Family Physicians (AAFP), American College of Physicians (ACP), and American Academy of Pediatrics (AAP).

The son of Quaker missionaries in West Africa, Paul Grundy, MD, becomes IBM's missionary for the *medical home* — gathering believers and championing a future where as many people as possible have a *Familiar Physician* backed by solid *inside the exam room* team care.

If we can achieve this goal, the two IBM physicians note, it will be a victory for primary care doctors who have prepared well, a victory for the patient-physician relationship and a huge leap forward for American health care.

In preparing *The Familiar Physician* for publication, we met with Dr. Grundy in Washington and asked him to take us back a few years and share with us the most persuasive appeals he and Dr. Sepúlveda made as the movement gains speed.

"We told anyone who would listen that IBM no longer wants to buy care from a system that does not manage our population."

"this is the elephant in the room: the affordability gap"

"America's health care crisis is hitting every family and every community. In the past ten years, every single cent of increases in labor pay has been drained off into health care."

"Doctors and hospitals get paid for having sicker patients. We get paid more if our patients have more treatments. At IBM, we decided that we were

AMERICA'S CHAMPIONS OF PRIMARY CARE

"Tenacious, passionate, persistent, bright, savvy in working relationships — Paul is the humble guy with the really big heart. He has shaped a movement that is transforming our system."

— **Bert Miuccio**, Director of Business Development, TransforMed doing a pretty dumb thing in the way we bought our health care. We were buying an episode of care."

And people cannot afford the care. "This is the elephant in the room. The affordability gap," Dr. Grundy adds.

Dr. Sepúlveda and Dr. Grundy meet over the next few months with the leadership of the primary care societies. Joining the movement quickly are key primary care leaders like Dr. Michael S. Barr of the American College of Physicians, who met them in Philadelphia and Dr. Douglas Henley of the American Academy of Family Physicians who met with them in Washington, DC," Dr. Grundy recalls.

Dr. Henley currently serves as the executive vice president and CEO of the American Academy of Family Physicians, with over 105,900 family physician and medical student members.

Dr. Barr is the Senior Vice President for Medical Practice for the American College of Physicians. The American College of Physicians (ACP) is a national organization of internal medicine physicians (internists). With 133,000 members, ACP is the largest medical-specialty organization and second-largest physician group in the United States.

Both of these physician leaders continue to champion primary care physicians as the backbone of America's health care system.

AMERICA'S CHAMPIONS OF PRIMARY CARE

"He's a visionary can-do type of person. Dr. Paul Grundy is not just about improving the health of patients; he is about doing so for entire populations. He wants, in his heart and in his soul, the right thing for people — to provide a better health care system versus a health care enterprise."

— **Douglas Henley, MD, FAAFP**, Executive Vice President and CEO, American Academy of Family Physicians, Vice Chair of the PCPCC Board of Directors

PART TWO

Theirs is a world of ideas

The reason I'm telling this story, and introducing its "present at the creation" characters, is that I believe when we learn how a vision is brought to life, it helps us understand where we might fit into that vision.

In the midst of any important social movement, as we are now with transforming American health care, the origins may get a little muddled. My hope is to add some clarity to the efforts that a relatively small number of people made on behalf of a much larger number.

At some point in their work they moved from the realm of vision and ideas into the world of reality.

When that moment occurred, or more precisely, began occurring, it was imperceptible to me. I was too bogged down with the frustration of being a primary care doctor and the efforts involved in saving my practice. I take solace in the fact that few others in or out of the field of medicine noticed either.

But it was happening nonetheless and this is the larger story that was developing around me and my individual efforts.

CHAPTER 4

BIRTH OF
THE COALITION

Dr. Martin Sepúlveda and Dr. Paul Grundy
Stage an Awkward Reunion

I f the process of turning the abstraction of the *medical home* into a solid form were part of a theatrical performance, this is the time when Dr. Sepúlveda and Dr. Grundy begin to share some of the play's best lines with several other actors.

At this point they are joined on the stage by Dr. Michael Barr, Dr. Douglas Henley, Dr. John Tooker, Navy Commander (CDR) Kevin Dorrance and Navy Lieutenant Commander (LCDR) Sunny Ramchandani. They are joined by Dr. John Crosby, Dr. Errol Alden and Dr. V. Fan Tait.

These physicians come from different backgrounds and experiences. What they share in common is their desire to innovate. Theirs is a world of ideas and they realize this may be the best opportunity they'll have to bring those ideas to life.

Dr. Douglas Henley

Dr. Douglas Henley of the American Association of Family Physicians remembers the birth of the coalition that brought the "House of Primary Care"

AMERICA'S CHAMPIONS OF PRIMARY CARE

"Dr. Martin Sepúlveda and Dr. Paul Grundy were integral to the early formation integral to the early formation of the PCPCC. Without industry and medicine working together with all the stakeholders, this would never have gotten off the ground."

— **Michael S. Barr, MD, M.B.A., FACP**, Senior Vice President, Division of Medical Practice, American College of Physicians into the room — internal medicine, pediatrics, family practice and osteopathic medicine — as having its origins in 2004.

It is that year that the AAFP, along with the other primary care organizations published the results of an extensive 2-½ year study entitled the Future of Family Medicine.

Dr. Henley explains that this key report was all about "the role, place and purpose of family medicine in the 21st century."

"This study demonstrated that the future of family medicine was untenable unless the system changed and the discipline of family medicine also changed. We called it then a "new model of care."

So it is in in 2005, that Dr. Douglas Henley meets Dr. Paul Grundy.

"Out of the clear blue sky he sent me an email about what Dr. Martin Sepúlveda and he were contemplating at IBM."

"It became obvious to the two of them and ultimately to the management of IBM that the reason American health care expenses are so much higher than other nations is that there is a much stronger primary care system abroad among the developed democracies."

"It didn't hurt either that Dr. Sepúlveda is a general internist by training and Dr. Grundy a preventive medicine specialist," Dr. Henley adds.

Momentum for the *medical home* idea continued at a brisk pace.

Dr. Michael Barr

In January 2006, Michael Barr, MD, MBA and Jack Ginsburg, the ACP director of Policy Analysis and Research, published a monograph entitled *A Patient-Centered, Physician-Guided Model of Health Care*. The Board of Regents quickly approved the paper.

In the same time frame, the American College of Physicians released a pivotal report entitled *State of the Nation's Health Care 2006: Proposals to Avert Looming Collapse of Primary Care*.

"We all wanted to take this even further," Dr. Barr recalls.

So in April 2006, the first action meeting with Dr. Martin Sepúlveda and Dr. Paul Grundy was held at a scientific session being held in Philadelphia.

"We learned of IBM's positions on primary care concerns, the issues of cost, physician shortages, and the need for professional societies to collaborate," Dr.

"THE IMMINENT COLLAPSE"

Sometimes, the language we use to describe a situation and get people's attention hits the mark. The way we shape the need for urgency itself becomes a catalyst for change.

Then, as now, Dr. Barr explains, Bob Doherty of the American College of Physicians plays a key role in solidifying the clear need to change so that this vision could be realized and why policymakers "need to be concerned about the imminent collapse of primary care in the United States."

Barr notes. "And we saw how all of it fit in with our parallel concerns about the potential collapse of primary care in the United States."

A short time later, in May of 2006, Dr. Barr had the opportunity to present the *medical home* model to the IBM team at the New York headquarters.

Dr. Barr vividly recalls this meeting as a pivotal point in a partnership between stakeholders who weren't always aligned in their direction.

"Dr. Martin Sepúlveda and Dr. Paul Grundy were key forces early on in the development of the *medical home*. Their advocacy, their efforts, even their cajoling at times to bring the professional societies together were defining moments in what I think is an important arc in the trajectory of health care in the U.S. It was, ultimately, the four societies and IBM who moved this forward."

"It's a great story of collaboration by industry, payors, health systems, providers and researchers."

I think it's worth noting that the American College of Physicians has a diverse membership in that over half of its members are internal sub-specialists. So they had to put aside any differences they might have. The leadership of the ACP, bringing the entire organization together to unite behind the *medical home*, has been a big factor in the success of the movement.

It's also important to remember, as Dr. Barr reminds us, that the *medical home* is not a model that was borrowed from another field. It doesn't have any direct analogy in the high reliability organizations that health care sometimes looks to for inspiration. It was developed by the medical profession, based on evidence, strengthened by the experience of the pediatrics field beginning in 1967 and shaped by Dr. Ed Wagner's Chronic Care Model and the MacColl Center for Health Care Innovation at the Group Health Research Institute in Seattle, all with a boost from IBM.

These early efforts and the dialogues they established help lead to a seminal gathering designated as the "Change of Covenant" meeting.

Dr. Ed Wagner had established the MacColl Center for Health Care Innovation in 1992, developing the Chronic Care Model with Dr. Michael von Korff, an evidence-based framework for health care that makes a big impact on the evolution of the *medical home*.

Dr. Henley then attended their first meeting in Washington, DC, a workshop, with Dr. John Tooker, CEO of the American College of Physicians and Dr. Michael Barr. Bob Doherty of the American College of Physicians was a key member of this team as was Rosi Sweeney of the American Academy of Family Physicians.

"Dr. Tooker and Dr. Barr teamed their efforts in the same way as Dr. Grundy and I," notes Dr. Sepúlveda.

Those early conversations quickly led them to bring in the Osteopathic and Pediatric groups as well, Dr. Henley recalls. This collaboration then led to the seminal gathering which they called the "Change of Covenant" meeting.

The pediatricians were the specialists that had already proven the *medical home* model works by every measure, having embraced the model as early as 1967.

Drs. Sepúlveda and Grundy note other key members of the team:

Errol Alden, MD, the CEO of the American Academy of Pediatrics and Dr. V. Fan Tait were key players in the movement.

"We also reached out to the American Osteopathic Association. We met with Shawn Martin and Dr. John Crosby and they became quick and powerful supporters of the *medical home* and subsequently, the PCPCC," Dr. Grundy recalls.

Martin then served as Director of Government Relations and Health Policy and Director of Socioeconomic Affairs at the American Osteopathic Association.

John B. Crosby, JD, is the Executive Director of the American Osteopathic Association that represents more than 100,000 osteopathic physicians (DOs) and osteopathic medical students.

"Much of the early legwork was effectively carried out by Edwina Rogers from ERISA, Rosemarie Sweeney from AAFP, Shawn Martin of AOA and Robert Doherty, the Senior Vice President of Governmental Affairs and Public Policy for ACP," Dr. Grundy notes.

The Seven *Joint Principles*

As the historic "Change of Covenant" meeting is being conceived, the four primary care societies create a special group to draft the vital *Joint Principles of the Patient-Centered Medical Home*. This would be the guiding document the primary care physicians would offer to the stakeholders of health care in America.

Rosemarie Sweeney, the American Academy of Family Physician's long-term vice president of advocacy, worked with Dr. Michael Barr and ACP's Bob

Doherty to complete the First Draft of the *Seven Joint Principles of the Patient-Centered Medical home.*

Rosemarie had been present at the very first meeting IBM held with Dr. Henley of the AAFP.

The collaborative work that is done during 2006 leads to the first call for a Medicare *Medical Home* Demonstration in the Tax Relief and Health Care Act of 2006.

It is also important to note that 19 additional physician organizations joined the primary care physician groups endorsing the *Joint Principles* as a result of considerable effort to explain the model. The gathering of like believers soon shifted to a different focus.

This *Joint Principles* document is quite significant because it is not only guiding the development of a newly organized health care system in America today, but in other nations who seek to improve their health care system, such as China.

As the four major associations of primary care physicians are fine-tuning the *Principles*, "it became obvious that this could not just be about the primary groups and IBM, a larger coalition was needed," Dr. Henley observes.

Birth of the Coalition

Led by Dr. Sepúlveda, IBM hosted the "Change of Covenant" conversation in the fall of 2006 in IBM's Washington, DC facility.

Gathered were Fortune 100 health care buyers, companies like Dell, Boeing, GM, Walgreens, Exxon, and Wells Fargo. Representatives from TRICARE, the federal Office of Personnel Management, the Department of Defense, Health and Human Services, insurance companies, physician associations, think tanks, pharmaceutical manufacturers, politicians and government leaders also attended.

Dr. Douglas Henley who was at this historic gathering remembers what it felt like to be in the room. "At that meeting you had the four major primary care organizations and a real cross section of American health care in the broadest sense. And then there was IBM, I mean what bigger brand can you get, speaking the same language with physicians, all making the case for primary care which we had been advocating for years."

A POWERFUL COALITION OF SUPPORT ASSEMBLES FOR THE *MEDICAL HOME* MODEL AND PRIMARY CARE

The PCMH care model is supported by the major primary care physician groups, including:

American Academy of Pediatrics
American Academy of Family Physicians
American College of Physicians
American Osteopathic Association

as well as 19 additional physician organizations:

American Academy of Hospice and Palliative Medicine
American Academy of Neurology
American College of Cardiology
American College of Chest Physicians
American College of Osteopathic Family Physicians
American College of Osteopathic Internists
American Geriatrics Society
American Medical Association
American Medical Directors Association

American Society of Addiction Medicine

American Society of Clinical Oncology

Association of Professors of Medicine

Association of Program Directors in Internal Medicine

Clerkship Directors in Internal Medicine

Infectious Diseases Society of America

Society for Adolescent Medicine

Society of Critical Care Medicine

Society of General Internal Medicine

The Endocrine Society

The Patient-Centered Primary Care Collaborative (PCPCC) is the nation's leading coalition dedicated to advancing an effective and efficient health system built on a strong foundation of primary care and the patient-centered medical home (PCMH). The PCPCC achieves its mission through the work of our five **Stakeholder Centers**, led by experts and thought leaders who are dedicated to transforming the U.S. health care system through delivery reform, payment reform, patient engagement, and employee benefit redesign. Today, PCPCC's membership represents more than 1,000 *medical home* stakeholders and supporters throughout the U.S.

AMERICA'S CHAMPIONS OF PRIMARY CARE

"This is a watershed, historic moment," said AAFP president Larry Fields, MD of Ashland, Ky. "It's the first time a large employer and a medical specialty society have collaborated to design a cost efficient, quality, affordable health care system for employees."

— **Sheri Porter**, AAFP News Now,
American Academy of Family Physicians

"It all seemed somehow self-serving when voiced alone. But not anymore."

The "Triple Aim"

The discussion, according to Dr. Henley, centered around how we can re-invest in delivering what is later named the "Triple Aim": improving the experience of care, improving the health of the population and reducing per capita cost of health care.

Later, Drs. Donald M. Berwick, Thomas W. Nolan and John Whittington published *The Triple Aim: Care, Health, And Cost* in Health Affairs in May of 2008.

Dr. Michael Barr describes the energy of that meeting as urgent.

"We were excited to see all the diverse stakeholders in the room," he recalled. "There was the sense that if we don't change this now, we may never get a better chance to improve patient care."

"There was a healthy discourse on the model, how it differed from the disease management model and then questions — such as, 'how do we know which practices are doing this?' This led to the development of NCQA, Joint Commission and URAC *medical home* practice recognitions and accreditations." The Accreditation Association for Ambulatory Health Care (AAAHC) in 2009 introduced the first accreditation program for *medical homes* to include an on-site survey.

Dr. Paul Grundy recalls that at the very end of the meeting, Kathleen Angel from Dell said "that is all very well and good. We love the *Principles* but 'where is the 8" by 10" glossy' describing it from a health care plan perspective so we can buy it?' " Kathleen Angel, Executive Director, Global Benefits and Mobility at Dell Inc. was honored in 2013 with the prestigious National Business Group on Health Award.

So after that gathering, it was clear that a lot of work remained to be done.

"For those of us in primary care," Dr. Henley recalls, "this meeting was amazing and yet appropriately challenging. We had the notion of the *medical home*. We didn't have the Patient-Centered Medical Home term yet — but we were close to that and the *Principles* made it clear that primary care needed to be paid differently and better to sustain this new model."

DR. MARGARET CHAN
DIRECTOR-GENERAL OF THE WORLD HEALTH ORGANIZATION

"Primary care is our best hope for the future. Family doctors are our rising stars for the future.

Out of the ashes built up by highly specialized, dehumanized, and commercialized medical care, family medicine rises like a phoenix, and takes flight, spreading its comprehensive spectrum of light, with the promise of a rainbow.

This is the ancient historical covenant between doctors and patients, and this is where the health and medical professions need to return. I encourage all of you to continue to cultivate the human side of medicine.

—**Dr. Margaret Chan**, June 2013

At this point there was some appropriate push back from the payors who wanted to see data. They asked to see demonstrations that showed the Patient-Centered Medical Home model could deliver lower costs.

So subsequently, many conversations were initiated with the specialty societies convening the groups or encouraging others to convene the payors since they could not convene themselves due to the perception of collusion.

Dr. Barr recalls that ACP convened meetings, and encouraged others such as business groups, ACP Chapters, and regional entities to support practice transformation. Medical Advantage Group — Michigan, and HealthTeamWorks came about, as did other national players such as Southwind from the Advisory Board Company and TransforMed.

"A group of us huddled right after that fall 2006 meeting. We understood that the answer is to create a broad-based coalition to drive support and create pilot programs for the Patient-Centered Medical Home," Dr. Grundy notes.

Dr. Barr also remembers one major takeaway from that meeting.

"We couldn't do it without more stakeholders involved," he notes.

At that moment, literally a few minutes after the meeting concluded, the PCPCC is born.

Dr. Ted Epperly

But one of the key champions of the *medical home* movement had a major premonition that this moment would be historic.

"When Dr. Sepúlveda and Dr. Grundy had their very first meeting with the American Academy of Family Physicians, Dr. Ted Epperly was on the Board and a key supporter from the earliest days of this movement. He championed the cause later as President and then Chairman of the AAFP and later wrote the seminal book *"Fractured: America's broken health care system and what we must do to heal it."*

Dr. Epperly remembers the first meeting clearly.

"It absolutely did feel like we were making history at this moment. When Drs. Sepulveda and Grundy came into our board meeting, laid out the background of their worldwide research and said 'we want to partner with you in primary care to help transform the U.S health care system', I got goosebumps," Dr. Epperly recalls.

"I was astounded," Dr. Epperly continues.

"We had been calling out in the dark until this moment. When IBM, unsolicited, came to us it was a frozen moment in time I will never forget. I saw the vision unfold, and it was crystal clear to me at that moment.

"here comes this wave of reason"

"I knew then that this is the way we would transform the largest sector of the American economy and how this would become a vehicle for major transformation. This was the most historic and powerful moment of my professional life."

"I just couldn't believe it," Dr. Epperly says.

"Here comes this wave of reason. It's one thing when the AAFP or ACP or other doctors groups advocate change. But it's another when IBM, a worldwide source of credible information, comes at it passionately.

"And the beauty of this, once we viewed it through the lens of these passionate IBM physicians, is that there really is no competing model. This is it. This is what fixes American health care. There are not eight other models to choose from. The *medical home* is working all over the globe — it's the re-emergence and re-awakening of the focus on primary care."

"Dr. Paul Grundy is the Johnny Appleseed of our time," quips Dr. Ted Epperly, one of the early leaders of the *medical home* movement and author of *"Fractured: America's broken health care system and what we must do to heal it."*

"He is relentless, throwing out those little apple seeds all over America — he is the true Johnny Appleseed for the United States in regards to health care reform!"

"We couldn't have had a better thought partner. We are in full alignment in the sense of social justice the *medical home* brings to American health care. It is right and noble to deliver a system of care set up for what the patients need, what's right for people, one that offers both cost control and social justice," Dr. Epperly notes.

The Seven Joint Principles of the
Patient-Centered Medical Home

In February 2007 the four major primary care physician associations, representing over 300,000 physicians, endorsed the Joint Principles of the Patient-Centered Medical Home, including the American Academy of Family Physicians (AAFP), American Academy of Pediatrics (AAP), American College of Physicians (ACP), and the American Osteopathic Association (AOA).

THE *JOINT PRINCIPLES*

- **Personal physician:** each patient has an ongoing relationship with a personal physician trained to provide first contact, and continuous and comprehensive care.
- **Physician directed medical practice**: the personal physician leads a team of individuals who collectively take responsibility for the ongoing care of each patient.
- **Whole person orientation:** the personal physician is responsible for providing all the patient's health care needs or taking responsibility for appropriately arranging care with other qualified professionals. This includes care for all stages of life; acute care; chronic care; preventive services and end of life care.
- **Care is coordinated and/or integrated:** care is coordinated across all elements of the complex health care system (e.g., subspecialty care, hospitals, home health agencies, nursing homes) and the patient's community (e.g., family, public and private community-based services). Care is facilitated by registries, information technology, health information exchange and other means to assure that patients get the indicated care when and where they need and want it in a culturally and linguistically appropriate manner.
  - ◊ Evidence-based medicine and clinical decision-support tools guide decision-making.
  - ◊ Physicians are accountable for continuous quality improvement through voluntary engagement in performance measurement and improvement.

◊ Patients actively participate in decision-making and feedback is sought to ensure patients' expectations are being met.

◊ Information technology is utilized appropriately to support optimal patient care, performance measurement, patient education, and enhanced communication.

◊ Practices go through a voluntary recognition process by an appropriate non-governmental entity to demonstrate that they have the capabilities to provide patient-centered services consistent with the *medical home* model.

◊ Patients and families participate in quality improvement activities at the practice level.

- **Enhanced access to care** is available through systems such as open scheduling, expanded hours and new options for communication between patients, their personal physician, and practice staff.

- **Payment appropriately recognizes the added value** provided to patients who have a Patient-Centered Medical Home. The payment structure should be based on the following framework:

  ◊ Reflect the value of physician and non-physician staff patient-centered care management work — tasks that fall outside of the face-to-face visit.

  ◊ Pay for services associated with coordination of care both within a given practice and between consultants, ancillary providers, and community resources.

  ◊ Support adoption and use of health information technology for quality improvement.

  ◊ Support provision of enhanced communication access such as secure e-mail and telephone consultation.

  ◊ Recognize the value of physician work associated with remote monitoring of clinical data using technology.

  ◊ Allow for separate fee-for-service payments for face-to-face visits. (Payments for care management services that fall outside of the face-to-face visit, as described above, should not result in a reduction in the payments for face-to-face visits).

◊ Recognize case mix differences in the patient population being treated within the practice.

◊ Allow physicians to share in savings from reduced hospitalizations associated with physician-guided care management in the office setting.

◊ Allow for additional payments for achieving measurable and continuous quality improvements.

CHAPTER 5

A NATIONAL CAMPAIGN BEGINS

Dr. Grundy Steps Up

Following that historic gathering, the pace quickens.

On October 15, 2007, representatives from seven of the nation's most prominent health benefits companies — Aetna, Blue Cross Blue Shield Association, CIGNA, Humana, MVP Health Care, UnitedHealthcare, and WellPoint, Inc. join in support of patient care improvements led by the Patient Centered Primary Care Collaborative (PCPCC).

So now, IBM has started a rally. On board are the four primary physician associations, national employers and their associations, quality advocacy groups, academic centers, consumer advocacy groups and now the major health plans weigh in powerfully for the *medical home.*

Dr. Grundy notes that this was a pivotal moment in the movement. And one key physician spoke up and placed it in perspective for everyone.

"I will never forget where Dr. Sam Nussbaum of Wellpoint was sitting and what he said in that very first meeting."

"We went around the room and Dr. Nussbaum is the first to speak passionately about the importance of this moment. 'We have got to do this. Our nation needs it. It has to be done!' " Dr. Nussbaum said.

Dr. Grundy recalls that this was the break point in the action, the tipping point, the place where the whole conversation changed."

The companies' support came in advance of the PCPCC's Call-To-Action Summit on Restructuring and Reintegrating Health Care Around the Patient, which took place in Washington, DC on November 7.

As Dr. Michael Barr remembers the sequence of events, "The insurance companies and payors gathered at the call of the American College of Physicians to design demonstration programs for the *medical home*. Horizon Blue Cross, Aetna, Independence Blue Cross and United all eagerly set about the task of working closely together to design reimbursement and payment strategies for the future.

The Commonwealth Fund led by Melinda Abrams, David Myers of the Agency for Healthcare Research and Quality and the Mathematica Policy Research team guided the largest initial funding for these demonstration projects.

Dr. Sam Nussbaum explains that "it was Paul's compelling leadership coupled to a vision which many of us shared and the creation of learning laboratories and pilots that were so impactful in advancing patient-centered primary care and the Patient-Centered Medical Home."

Katie Capps

Katherine Herring Capps of Health2 Resources helped shape the highly successful PCPCC membership campaign, while Dr. Paul Grundy carried the banner across the country and history was made.

"At first, it was just a few passionate people and very thin resources. But we had Paul, and we had Edwina Rogers from ERISA," Katie Capps recalls.

The ERISA Industry Committee (ERIC) in Washington, DC advocates the employee benefits and compensation interests of America's major employers.

"The PCPCC was incubated in the ERISA Industry Committee (ERIC). Edwina was then ERIC's vice president of health policy and an ardent supporter of the *medical home* model."

Katie Capps adds that Edwina Rogers became the founding executive director of the PCPCC, a position she held from 2006-2011.

"She worked with Paul and others to build a coalition committed to turning talk into action and vision into reality," according to Capps.

"Paul, Edwina and I sat together in the ERISA board room over several meetings to lay out an operational plan that included recruitment of membership

WHAT IS A *MEDICAL HOME*?

The *medical home* is best described as a model or philosophy of primary care that is patient-centered, comprehensive, team-based, coordinated, accessible, and focused on quality and safety. It has become a widely accepted model for how primary care should be organized and delivered throughout the health care system.

The "*medical home*" is not a place, but a philosophy of health and health care that encourages us to meet patients where they are, from the most simple to the most complex conditions. Its success is enhanced by health information technology and incentivized by smarter ways to pay for care. Above all: the *medical home* is not a final destination. It is a framework for achieving primary care excellence so that care is received in the right place, at the right time, and the manner that best suits a patient's needs.

Features of the Medical Home

The *medical home* is an approach to the delivery of primary care that is:

- Patient-centered: A partnership among practitioners, patients, and their families ensures that decisions respect patients' wants, needs, and preferences, and that patients have the education and support they need to make decisions and participate in their own care.

- Comprehensive: A team of care providers is wholly accountable for a patient's physical and mental health care needs, including prevention and wellness, acute care, and chronic care.
- Coordinated: Care is organized across all elements of the broader health care system, including specialty care, hospitals, home health care, community services and supports.
- Accessible: Patients are able to access services with shorter waiting times, "after hours" care, 24/7 electronic or telephone access, and strong communication through health IT innovations.
- Committed to quality and safety: Clinicians and staff enhance quality improvement through the use of health IT and other tools to ensure that patients and families make informed decisions about their health.

Agency for Healthcare Research & Quality:

*http://pcmh.ahrq.gov/portal/server.pt/community/pcmh__home/1483/what_is_pcmh_*

and leadership through various PCPCC 'Centers,' giving voice to the variety of issues that would arise over the coming years."

Paul addressed the question, " 'how do we pay for value?' ."

"This is a real supply-side strategy for key decision makers," she says.

His call, according to Katie Capps, brought together "like-minded people who were willing to excel during the chaos" going on at the time.

"...a different health trajectory for America"

"The PCPCC was never designed to be a Washington, DC-based advocacy agency. Its purpose was different — it always was intended to make a true and noticeable change, to make a dent in the Universe. They built upon exemplary practices in the market, never letting 'Perfect' be the enemy of 'Good' ."

For the next several years, Katie Capps becomes a key player in the development of this powerful coalition, designing an effective campaign, which would forge a different health trajectory for America.

Ultimately, nearly a thousand diverse organizational stakeholders in medicine are now all behind a great idea — the *medical home* model. We hope this concept will be the saving grace of primary care.

Christopher Nohrden

Dr. Paul Grundy's key operational team in the formative years is headed by Chris Nohrden.

"I am, of course, proud of my role in helping to inaugurate and establish the PCPCC," Chris Nohrden says.

"But, I'm also happy to have been part of the dialogue with other self-insured employers about how the *medical home* model provides them value."

Because visionary companies like IBM and other major self-insured employers are demanding this change to their health insurance plans, many will be requiring their payors to reimburse the primary care *medical home* model.

"There won't be significant changes in health care delivery until we change the way we pay for care," he notes.

From my vantage point in Newport News, VA, I am becoming excited about this groundbreaking direction. While this may indeed be one of the few times that the entire medical community has united on anything, I hope and pray it will last, because this will help save the primary care doctors of America from the coming perfect storm, if they prepare for it well.

Dr. Grundy is a master at coming into a room and bringing everyone together behind a single idea that can unite them — even people immersed in heated competition with each other.

Under the umbrella of the Patient-Centered Primary Care Collaborative, Dr. Grundy and society leaders from AAFP, ACP, AOA, and AAP as well as all of the involved staff begin their work. Their goal is to unite everyone who is a stakeholder in reform around this central idea of the primary doctor once again becoming the backbone of medical care in America.

This powerful, articulate physician gathers believers and champions a future where every American citizen has a *Familiar Physician*, a care team and a "*medical home.*"

If we can achieve this goal, it will be a victory for internists. It will be a victory for pediatricians. It will be a victory for osteopathic physicians and for family practitioners. It will be a victory for the patient-physician relationship and a huge leap forward for American health care.

PART THREE

This is called momentum

As the primary evangelist of the *medical home*, ground soldier in a quest envisioned by Dr. Martin Sepúlveda and IBM, president of the Collaborative and champion of the primary care doctor — Dr. Paul Grundy invests athletic energy into a tireless cross country campaign and gathers hundreds and hundreds of key organizations representing every stakeholder in medicine.

And then hundreds more.

So now about a thousand organizational voices representing millions of health care professionals echo the call for this change, and the "PCPCC is taking it to the next level — bringing together a lot of people doing really great things to transform the delivery of health care — a real success story in the value of connectivity," Chris Nohrden says.

This is called momentum.

CHAPTER 6

A DENT IN
THE UNIVERSE
The Tipping Point Is Reached

T he national media begins noticing Dr. Paul Grundy. Major magazines interview him. He goes on an extensive speaking tour. He talks with governors, insurers, military medicine gatherings, physicians groups, health care associations, universities, and worldwide forums offering his belief in the Patient-Centered Medical Home to any group that will listen.

"convincing information flows from the podium"

Dr. Grundy is now navigating a course to bring together the major players in American health care. That begins with the medical establishment but extends further.

Virtually every group and individual he encounters shares the belief that the primary care physician is the foundation for the future of the American health care system.

"What has made a difference is connecting people," he modestly observes. "This isn't about changing people's minds. It's about helping them speak together in a louder voice."

We asked Dr. Grundy about pivotal moments that helped drive him forward in this effort. He tells us that one of his inspirations is his deep friendship with Dr. Bob Graham, the former vice president of the American Academy of Family Physicians.

Dr. Paul Grundy and his mentor Dr. Bob Graham

"Bob is a living example of what I needed to do."

Dr. Grundy remembers this moment vividly.

"It was a breakfast before the very first public meeting of the Collaborative just after the PCPCC was formed, a meeting of the early adopters — physician practices like Dr. Peter Anderson's, which I was going to be addressing."

"Over breakfast, I was telling Bob about the data around of the importance of primary care. Bob looked at me and said 'that is not what this audience, the fervent believers in the power of PCMH care, are looking for' ."

Dr. Grundy said, "So I asked him what they are looking for and will never forget his answer."

" 'They don't need to be convinced," he said. They need to know someone is willing to get out in front of this idea. They are looking for a leader. They want to know you believe what they are doing is important, powerful, needed and that you are willing to both lead them and to empower them' ."

"This is about social change, Bob went on to say. "Social entrepreneurship, capacity building. You have the folks that are ready to step up, work hard, deliver change and they want to know someone who they can look up to is leading them' ."

THE EIGHT LAWS OF SOCIAL CHANGE

Dr. Grundy shares some thoughts he had learned from the Quakers beginning as a child.

"These rules are meant to apply to fighting violence in communities," he says, but they can have import in and provide guidance in other areas, too. "Individuals and small groups can change history by practicing these eight laws which are really the eight laws of social change."

1. Individuals and groups must share a common purpose or intent — consensus.
2. Individuals and groups may have goals, but must not be attached to "cherished" outcomes.
3. The goal may not be reached in the lifetime of the participants.
4. Accept and be OK with the idea that you might not get credit for the success of a goal.
5. Each person in the group must have equal status in spite of any hierarchies.
6. Members must forswear violence by word, thought and act.
7. Private selves consistent with public postures.
8. People are not exploitable resources. People are what make change happen and the most important element.

And remember

- Do not seek to defeat and humiliate opponents. Instead seek to make friends and awaken a sense of shame over injustice.
- Do not go after individuals, rather the evil systems that victimize both the oppressed and the oppressor.
- We avoid internal violence of spirit. We refuse to hate our opponent. An "eye for an eye" leaves everyone blind.
- Love that offers creative understanding and seeks nothing in return.
- Love your enemies — this transforms the soul of your opponent.
- Have faith in the future believing the universe is on the side of justice.
- No lie can live forever.

empowering believers

That brought the whole notion of social change back to Dr. Grundy.

"And it changed my approach. I recalled the Eight Laws of Social Change from my Quaker roots," Dr. Grundy remembers.

The meeting with Bob Graham changed Dr. Grundy's approach.

"Instead of trying to convince people by the use of data, I began to point out those in the crowd who are living it. Physicians like Dr. Peter Anderson from Virginia, Dr. Joseph Mambu at Lower Gwynedd, Pennsylvania, Navy CDR Kevin Dorrance, Dr. Don Klitgaard from Iowa, Dr. David Hanekom of North Dakota leading the charge from Blue Cross, Julie Schilz at Anthem leading the work from Colorado, Dr. John Blair from the Hudson Valley."

"The shift in my thinking took me away from feeling I have to make the data so clear and understood that everyone will believe — to empowering those who already believe. Now I seek to help them create their small, sometimes isolated but important successes, to connect them, to help them turn something powerful but small, obscure, into something big."

"To lead to me meant taking the point of view of Dr. Martin Sepúlveda, Tom Bodelheimer, Ed Wagner, Peter Anderson and connect them — to help tip over into something big and significant."

So how did it manifest itself when I wasn't at the podium? Once someone was identified to me as being a leader in the *medical home*, he or she would not infrequently get phone calls from me.

he works without fanfare, knowing that this
quiet advocacy is what will bring us together

"I would also champion these leaders to the working press," Dr. Grundy continues, suggesting to reporters practitioners who would make great interviews. "I recall referring Julie Rovner of NPR who wanted to see PCMH in practice so I referred them to Dr. Peter Anderson and to Dr. David Howes at Martins Point Group Practice in Maine."

"I did a lot with the Department of Defense at this time, often connecting civilian and military leadership when the DoD was looking for folks with experience in team-based PCMH level care. This sort of leadership was happening all over the country."

"guide the dynamic of the little things"

"Leading meant to me, as I understood it from Bob that day, to guide the dynamic of the little things that cause changes that have big effects."

When Dr. Grundy shared this story, a light bulb went off. I have always wondered if Dr. Grundy had suggested my *Family Team Care* expertise to the U.S. Army, which eventually gave us a major training grant for ambulatory care centers.

He works without fanfare, knowing that this quiet advocacy is what will bring us together.

And I make a mental note that what he is accomplishing takes enormous passion and dedication. He never stops moving, never stops recruiting believers, and never stops acknowledging everyone who is a stakeholder in American medicine. He speaks everywhere he is invited. He brings data. Convincing information flows from the podium. He tells stories from around the world. Every aspect of his message is about becoming patient-centered again. He introduces and praises those already engaged.

"…the tipping point is reached"

And Washington begins to listen.

Stephanie Bouchard, Managing Editor for Healthcare Finance News quoted Dr. Grundy in a powerful article on the *medical home* model, "the one thing everyone in health care can agree upon."

The current health care system is a "graveyard," she quotes PCPCC President Paul Grundy, M.D, but "he has a roadmap that will take the country to the Promised Land."

The tipping point is reached.

We got here with inspiration. And hard work. But who inspired the physicians who inspired us? One of the requests we made of Dr. Sepúlveda and Dr. Grundy was to ask them to share with us who inspired them.

The *medical home* begins in practice in Hawaii and is led by pediatrician Calvin C.J. Sia, MD He develops innovative programs to improve the quality

AMERICA'S CHAMPIONS OF PRIMARY CARE

"Paul had a very important role in helping us understand the *medical home* model, in determining what specific aspects of the *medical home* model should be incorporated into policy, and galvanizing employers and the payors to drive demand for *medical home* practices"

—Bob Kocher, MD

Former Special Assistant to the President for Health Care and Economic Policy, National Economic Council (2009—2010)

Now a Visiting Scholar at the Brookings Institution and a venture capitalist at Venrock of medical care for children in the United States and Asia. His *medical home* model for pediatric care and early childhood development takes root in several Asian countries in 2003.

This is the birth of the *medical home* concept for primary care, to which Dr. Sia attached the slogan, "Every Child Deserves a *Medical Home.*"

Dr. Martin Sepúlveda knows him well.

"Dr. Sia is one of two physicians who continuously inspired me in my vision and career," notes Dr. Sepúlveda. "He is the guy I would bounce ideas off of, call when I was frustrated, and go to for counsel."

'The other doctor who inspired me is Dr. Barbara Starfield, who many people admire as one of the most powerful forces in primary care. We would meet and talk and brainstorm often."

Dr. Sepúlveda recalls in the very early days right after the first organizational gatherings, Dr. Starfield is attending a large meeting of stakeholders, which included a lot of governmental players. She begins to feel the meeting drift toward the usual conversation at the time, physician compensation. In those early days, the issue of payment for service was impeding the real mission and purpose, he notes.

"I recall she stood up halfway through this meeting and shouted 'If this is all about higher payment for primary caregivers, I am out of here' ," Dr. Sepúlveda fondly recalls.

Today, the PCPCC honors the memory of Dr. Starfield with the *Barbara Starfield Award*, given each year for primary care leadership at the organization's annual meeting.

"Dr. Barbara Starfield was about people, active living, helping families fulfill their potential. She was about the hero physicians and nurses who are out there making the changes we need to make," he adds.

Dr. Grundy also pays tribute to the work of Dr. Starfield, and to the major contributions of Dr. Karen Davis as well.

"We built upon the groundbreaking work of Dr. Starfield and Dr. Karen Davis," recalls Dr. Grundy.

Karen Davis PhD. is president of The Commonwealth Fund, a national philanthropy engaged in independent research on health and social policy issues. Dr. Davis is a nationally recognized economist, with a distinguished career in public policy and research. Today she is at Johns Hopkins Bloomberg School of Public Health.

We lost Dr. Starfield in 2011. People are most familiar with her work at Johns Hopkins School of Public Health, where she founded the Center for Primary Care Policy. She was the co-founder and first president of the *International Society for Equity in Health*, a scientific organization devoted to the dissemination of knowledge about the determinants of inequity in health and finding ways to eliminate them. Her work focused on quality of care, health status assessment, primary care evaluation, and equity in health.

Other seminal works were provided to us by Dr. Tom Bodenheimer.

"The Bodenheimer model called for a change of covenant, a very far-sighted vision from folks within the 'House of Primary Care' ," Dr. Grundy notes.

Dr. Grundy refers to the groundbreaking work on The Teamlet Model of Primary Care as published in 2007 by Thomas Bodenheimer, MD and Brian Yoshio Laing, BS.

"The work at the University of Utah and University of Washington set us up for success," he recalls.

The nation once again began to re-create medicine in America, with the primary care physician at the center.

Now we have to figure out just how the doctors could carry this additional weight without sinking in the mire.

Vermont *Blueprint's* Craig Jones, MD

As Craig Jones, MD the Executive Director of the acclaimed *Blueprint for Health*, for the state of Vermont says, "Dr. Paul Grundy may be the most knowledgeable in the United States about the state of health care in the U.S."

"He knows so much about this subject. He has an elegant vision and a critical mind; he sees the problem from here to there as well or as better than anyone I have even known. He can see the landscape of the entire country."

"His vision, his devotion to mission and his sense of purpose to the common good is helping to move us forward in all those respects," Dr. Jones adds.

As the nation is poised to re-invent the way we deliver medical care, this issue affects every man, woman and child in America. And the passionate members of the PCPCC can sense victory.

As the new Affordable Care Act and other reforms roll out over the next decade, the *medical home* vision is at the center of attention.

CHAPTER 7

MEANWHILE OUR TEAM ASSEMBLES A NEW MODEL

Creating Shelter Against the Perfect Storm

This important change looming with regard to the *medical home* model can have one of two results: they can save primary care doctors, or be a bit of bad weather in the perfect storm scenario currently descending on American physicians.

Now we have reached the moment in this narrative where the crossroads begins.

The Familiar Physician — Saving Your Doctor in the Era of Obamacare is concerned with what kind of transformation needs to happen for doctors, for their staff, for the way they inform and educate their patients, and for their leadership skills in order to make this new system work.

And I am energized and empowered to continue to help re-invent primary care delivery on a scale that fits our office.

America's new primary care pioneer, Dr. Grundy is now powering ahead, creating a robust strengthening of primary care — which he is absolutely convinced will be the brightest and best pathway for America to move away from its broken health care system.

IBM's ongoing examination of health care globally is an important springboard for Dr. Grundy's campaign aimed at leading the charge for reform with a more rigorous primary care model. The IBM findings of their global study show that more primary care access leads to a healthier population, which in turn leads to such macro and micro benefits as a better national economy and improved patient satisfaction — a basic formula with consistent confirmation.

Dr. Grundy's recruiting of stakeholders from across the private and public sectors to promote learning, awareness and innovation of the *medical home* model is changing everything for the better.

His timing in helping to execute Dr. Sepúlveda's strategic plan is perfect.

preserves the best

Meanwhile, back in Newport News, our small team is developing an evolving concept of organizing care in the medical office so that the perfect storm of health care reform doesn't overtake us. This new shaping of the consumer/patient/family experience preserves the best of what America can recall from the past — the vital, mutually respected and mutually appreciated relationship between a physician and her or his patient.

I am thrilled to see that our *Family Team Care* approach fits like the proverbial glove into the PCPCC *medical home* vision.

"…it only works if we rescue the primary care physicians "

Working from different levels of magnitude, though in similar ways, both Dr. Paul Grundy and I are pursuing the goal of rescuing the primary care physician, an effort which helps make the coming changes in health reform actually work, and work relatively quickly.

And part of what makes those changes work is restoring and maintaining the joy and pleasure of practicing medicine.

At some point, whether it's early or late in a medical career, every doctor understands why he or she goes into medicine. But more than any other medical specialty, primary care doctors chose this field because of the potential for trusting, confident relationships built over time with their patients.

I'm experiencing renewed excitement in my practice. And along with insightful and hard working staff, we are nearing the time when we'll be ready, compelled really, to get out and share what we've learned, sometimes through trial and error.

AMERICA'S CHAMPIONS OF PRIMARY CARE

"Paul has demonstrated time and time again by stepping up, taking the lead and inspiring us to always remember and place the patient at the center of everything we do."

— **Robert Dribbon**, Director of Health Care System Strategy for Merck, serves as Executive Committee Liaison for the PCPCC's Executive Committee

Before I decided to "take to the road" and approach the national stage of primary care medicine with our solution, I needed to better understand the power of collaboration. Dr. Paul Grundy gave me that example.

In fact, our *Family Team Care* is all about a new model of collaboration between a doctor and a nurse, between a team and a leader, between saving the best of what existed and merging it with a whole new process.

Dr. Paul Grundy continues to help shape the future of health care in America through a keen focus on collaboration.

Years and years of those sometimes-solitary road trips all over the nation pay off.

> ## "a fellow physician who knew of my work called me 'Paul Revere'. I like that."

Dr. Grundy is grateful that he is finding traction now and starting to get more recognition around the country, after years of rallying support for the Patient-Centered *Medical Home*.

"One summer, Dr. Grundy fondly recalls, "I was on a flight and happened to sit next to a fellow physician who was following 'my work' as he called it and he showed me the book *The Tipping Point* which I am humbled to said I had not read."

"See right here, he said to me, '*The law of the few* says that success of any kind of social epidemic is…heavily dependent on the involvement of people with a particular and rare set of social gifts. These people are *mavens* — experts in a particular field, and also *connecters*, known to and trusted by others, and who have wider connections to influential groups' ."

He said Paul Revere is such an example.

"Paul, see right here. You are the one — the *connector* and the *maven*. You are the Paul Revere of health care transformation."

That person Paul later told me was Dr. Rocky Martin, the dean of an osteopathic school and father of Dr. Sean Martin, now Director of Advocacy at the American Academy of Family Physicians.

While it was a friendly poke from a fellow passenger, the parallel with Henry Wadsworth Longfellow's poem, the vehicle by which most of us get our knowledge of Paul Revere and his famous ride, is intriguing.

In the poem, Revere tells a friend to prepare signal lanterns in the Old North Church in Boston to inform him if the British will attack by land or sea.

He would await the signal across the river in Charlestown and be ready to spread the alarm throughout Middlesex County, Massachusetts. The friend climbs up the steeple and soon sets up two signal lanterns, letting Revere know that the British are coming by sea. Revere rides his horse through Medford, Lexington, and Concord to warn the patriots.

Thus continues the ride of Dr. Paul Grundy, as an alarm, a plea for action, and a call to arms.

early *medical home* discussions

Dr. Grundy, in speaking before the 7th Annual World Health Care Congress, recalled the days when the *medical home* model was just being embraced.

"When we first brought this up, we had a round table discussion and the conversation centered on the Patient-Centered Medical Home concept in general and the name in particular.

"We discussed how the name works well in pediatrics as well as the military with its allusion to a home military base. But it doesn't play so well with the senior population because they may equate it with 'nursing home...' "

After considerable discussion it rolled out in the eight state pilot programs as "advanced primary care."

Dr. Grundy noted that as time passed, however, the benefits of the "Patient-Centered Medical Home" name outweighed any possible liabilities.

These pioneering physician leaders gave the nation a new direction for health care, and literally and figuratively, a new covenant.

They championed a new system of care, based on an old idea, that each patient has an ongoing relationship with a personal doctor trained to provide first contact, and continuous and comprehensive care.

Unlike Paul Revere's colonial adversaries, the perfect storm approaching American health care is coming both by land and by sea. Fortunately, dedicated people are shining a lantern that will help illuminate the reorganization of primary care.

By 2008, my practice is thriving and *Family Team Care* is becoming an example of how primary care physicians can make the kind of changes that improve the experience of medicine for themselves, their staffs and their patients.

Family Practice Management magazine features us. Dr. Paul Grundy invites me to speak about what we've accomplished in San Diego at the American Association of Family Physicians national conference.

The American Academy of Family Physicians is staking their whole future on the *medical home*," Dr. Terry McGeeney told an audience of physicians at that AAFP's Scientific Assembly in San Diego in September 2008.

Waiting my turn to speak, and hearing this strong assertion, I felt as if I had been called in to pinch hit in the seventh game of the World Series after having just come up from the minors.

Within minutes, I would soon be speaking at a national meeting for the first time in my professional career. To extend my World Series musings, I was definitely wondering if I was out of my league.

I needn't have been concerned. My message, one of a very personal example of how big ideas work on the ground level, was warmly received.

"we must always place the patient at the center of what we do"

By 2009, Dr. Paul Grundy is on a whirlwind national speaking circuit. His message on the potential for the *medical home* continues to inspire me and a growing number of physicians. Early in the year he brings that message to the Virginia Family Practice Conference.

It centers on preserving the primary care physician and the physician-patient relationship as one of the most powerful forces in medicine. Although his words connect with everyone in attendance, they are particularly meaningful to me because strengthening the physician-patient relationship, and the improved health outcomes that derive from it, is exactly where we have been focusing our efforts as a practice.

"We must always place the patient at the center of what we do," he goes on to tell the audience, and avoid the non-physician activities that end up wasting at least 40% of our time.

"Trust, communication, empowerment and the expectation that physicians will be properly compensated — these are the things," he reminded us, "that we have to put back into primary care medicine."

During the conference I told Dr. Grundy that I would devote myself to sharing what we have learned to help get the primary care field out of the mire, to embrace the *medical home* model and to make that model successful.

primary care doctors can transform their practice to *inside the exam room* team care

There are other team care systems being tried around the country, with varying degrees of success, using different staffing models and alternative processes. Pilot programs are trying out every conceivable method of re-designing the primary care provider's operations.

We're ahead of the curve on this re-design because we have been working on it for years. During that time, we begin sharing the approach we took *inside the exam room* and offer training to other primary care teams. What they tell us after the training is that they would never go back to the old way of practicing medicine.

What their results and feedback confirms, and what I see firsthand in my own practice, is that without re-structuring the primary care office, the *medical home* will not be successful.

first in Virginia

In April of 2009, our practice becomes the first primary care practice in Virginia to become certified as a *medical home* by the National Committee for Quality Assurance (NCQA).

In that same month, I receive an invitation to speak at the Brookings Institution, on rebuilding the primary care network in the United States. Brookings is America's oldest and most prestigious public policy organization. Dr. Paul Grundy had suggested my name.

I pause to reflect on the fact that I have come a long way from a struggling primary care practice with my nurses ready to quit. And it's a journey I don't take for granted.

CHAPTER 8

DR. GRUNDY BECOMES THE VOICE OF POSSIBILITY

What if everyone had a medical home?

During the early years of change, Dr. Martin Sepúlveda stayed on his plan. His long-standing and passionate belief in the *medical home* as the foundation for America's medical care is now a very real possibility.

Throughout this period he maintained an essential mentoring and supportive role. "The contribution I am making at this point is to provide both a sounding board and a key source of counseling to these visionaries in the field," he notes.

"When you are in active transformation, once you really get in the trenches, all kinds of complexities present themselves, and you need somebody keeping you on task. This mission control role is the one I chose to play, through dispassionate, objective feedback."

"I did that by visiting all the primary care organization boards, sharing my thoughts on the issues they needed to stay focused on, showing them where the potential minefields, the ones that always accompany rapid growth, could appear."

Doctors who have transformed their practices into *medical home*s are pleased, even a bit surprised at how well it is working for them and Dr. Bob Kocher has a good idea why.

Dr. Bob Kocher

Bob Kocher, MD, is a national health care leader and a key architect of health care reform.

"I have not heard of a single doctor who would go back (from the *medical home* model). This is a really, really better way. Currently, patients are clearly responsible to arrange all their care on their own."

Dr. Kocher compares the present medical system to the analogy of repairing your car by running all over town, gathering up the needed parts and then trying to put it all together by yourself. It just might not work, he notes.

And by the way, during the "repair work" the patient is usually sick, definitely not operating at 100%, and still making these important decisions.

"What I love about the *medical home* model is that you select a primary care doctor and that practice will work — with you at the center — to engage the entire health care system on your behalf. It's practical. It's coordinated. It's a much better patient experience with far better access, including practices that are open seven days a week, and same-day visits."

Dr. Kavita Patel

In preparing The *Familiar Physician*, we had the opportunity to talk with Dr. Kavita Patel at the end of another intense and busy day at Johns Hopkins. Dr. Patel is a leading expert in the area of health care policy.

"Dr. Paul Grundy is a guy with great ideas," Dr. Patel says.

Dr. Patel shares the moment she met Dr. Grundy.

"Dr. Paul Grundy is the voice of possibility"

"I remember well when we first met. Here he comes…kind of happy-go-lucky, with an 'ah shucks' persona and he begins our meeting by powerfully explaining that we know what the *medical home* concept is now; but then moving on to the potential, — the future and the power of the *medical home* model if we did this everywhere…"

"He offered, 'How would it feel to be a patient or a doctor in one of the *medical homes*? You really know your patients. Every patient seeing what they deserve — a physician they really know…' "

"I knew then that Dr. Paul Grundy is the voice of possibility," she concludes. Dr. Patel explains that his forming of the PCPCC was historic.

"His establishment of the PCPCC institutionalized a movement. I honestly don't know if people understand how he did this — or how do you go from that one idea to a coalition with over 1,000 organizations."

"No one knows how much effort went into that."

Dr. Martin Sepúlveda's involvement with the growing influence of the PCPCC included some suggestions along the way for governance and recruitment, nurturing and energizing the movement at key moments.

"I have a great deal of respect for Dr. Paul Grundy's leadership at PCPCC," he notes.

"Marci Nielsen, PhD, MPH, who joined the PCPCC as Chief Executive Officer in 2012, brought in a powerful patient focus," he notes, a feature that many *medical home* organizations often neglect, and which in turn has transitioned the PCPCC from a movement to a thought leadership organization.

DEVELOPMENT OF THE PATIENT-CENTERED MEDICAL HOME AND THE JOURNEY OF PETER ANDERSON, MD KEY CHRONOLOGICAL EVENTS

1967

American Academy of Pediatrics (AAP) introduces the *medical home* concept in an effort to improve and coordinate care for children with multiple/special needs.

1978

Dr. Peter Anderson graduates from University of Virginia Medical School.

1987

Surgeon General Everett Koop's seminal report calls for coordinated, family-centered, community-based care for children with special health care needs and their families.

2001

Institute of Medicine (IOM) calls for transformation of a "fundamentally flawed" U.S. health care system in the report *Crossing the Quality Chasm*.

2003

Dr. Peter Anderson begins a multi-year struggle to lift his once successful primary care practice out of the mire.

2004

In *The Future of Family Medicine Project* the primary care field proposes a new model of care, the "personal *medical home*."

2005

TransforMED is created as a subsidiary of American Academy of Family Physicians (AAFP) to implement The Future of Family Medicine.

2006

In January, Michael Barr, MD, MBA and Jack Ginsburg, the ACP director of Policy Analysis and Research, published a monograph entitled *A Patient-Centered, Physician-Guided Model of Health Care*. The Board of Regents quickly approved the paper.

2006

In April, the first vital meeting is held by Dr. Sepúlveda and Dr. Grundy with Dr. Michael S. Barr of the American College of Physicians.

2006

In May, Dr. Martin Sepúlveda makes an historic presentation to the AAFP Board offering up a strategy of strong primary care as a strategy to move forward.

2006

Medical home demonstration projects within Medicare are called for in the Tax Relief and Health Care Act, to be implemented by 2010.

2006

In August, the PCPCC is conceived at the home of Dr. Sepúlveda created by the IBM team and the "House of Primary Care," the AAFP, AAP, AOA and ACP.

2006

In the fall, an historic "Change of Covenant" meeting takes place in the IBM Building, hosted by Dr. Martin Sepúlveda. Following this meeting, IBM helped create the Patient-Centered Primary Care Collaborative (PCPCC), a group of large employers and the major primary care physician associations: American Osteopathic Association (AOA), American Academy of Family Physicians (AAFP), American College of Physicians (ACP), and American Academy of Pediatrics (AAP).

2006

PCPCC is officially launched in late 2006, when the ERISA Industry Committee (ERIC) was approached by IBM and other large national employers with the objective of reaching out to the primary care groups to facilitate improvements in patient-clinician relations, and create a more effective and efficient model of health care delivery. Edwina Rogers, who was then ERIC's vice president of health, became the founding executive director of the PCPCC.

2007

In February, four organizations — American Academy of Pediatrics (AAP), American Academy of Family Physicians (AAFP), American College of Physicians (ACP), and American Osteopathic Association (AOA) — jointly issue the *Joint Principles of the Patient-Centered Medical Home*.

2007

Teamlet Model of Primary Care published by Thomas Bodenheimer, MD

2007

The Patient-Centered Primary Care Collaborative is launched through an effort by several large national companies to improve patient-physician relationships and create a more effective and efficient model of health care delivery.

2007

National Committee for Quality Assurance (NCQA) launches the tool *Physician Practice Connections/Patient-Centered Medical Home*, which becomes the standard for PCMH recognition.

2007

As the civilian health care community gains traction, the initial planning and testing of the PCMH concept began in 2007 at the National Naval Medical Center (now the Walter Reed National Military Medical Center).

At Bethesda, two officers begin the full-scale effort to spearhead the change to the *medical home* model — CDR Kevin A. Dorrance, MC USN and LCDR Suneil "Sunny" Ramchandani, MC USN.

2008

Family Team Care organization led by Dr. Peter Anderson matures into a formal training model.

2008

Naval Commander Ramchandani met Dr. Paul Grundy in person for the first time in the Spring of 2008, when they asked IBM for support in developing some IT tools for the Navy's *medical home* program.

2008

Family Team Care, Dr. Peter Anderson's training organization, gains steam when national publication Family Practice Management publishes in July-August 2008 *"A New Approach to Making Your Doctor-Nurse Team More Productive — With proper training and delegation, your team can see more patients, deliver better care and feel more satisfied at work."* Peter Anderson, MD and Marc D. Halley, MBA. This relationship would soon evolve into a formal training collaboration for the health systems supported by Halley Consulting of Cleveland, Ohio.

2008

The Commonwealth Fund, Qualis Health, and MacColl Institute initiate a five-year demonstration project to assist safety net primary care clinics in becoming high-performing PCMHs — helping 65 community health centers in five states transform into Patient-Centered *Medical Home*s.

2008

The National Committee for Quality Assurance (NCQA) releases Physician Practice Connections (PCMH) standards.

2008

The VA adopts the *medical home* model for their eight million beneficiaries.

2008

The Patient-Centered Medical Home model is implemented at Edwards Air Force Base and Ellsworth Air Force Base.

2008

Center for *Medical Home* Improvement's *Medical Home* Index is developed.

2009

Accreditation Association for Ambulatory Health Care (AAAHC)'s Medical Home standards are released.

2009

In January, Dr. Paul Grundy speaks to the Virginia Family Practice Conference inspiring Dr. Peter Anderson to help transform America's primary care physicians.

2009

The Office of the Assistant Secretary of Defense (Health Affairs) directed MHS-wide *medical home* implementation. In September 2009, the United States Department of Defense issues HA Policy 09-015. Policy Memorandum Implementation of the "Patient-Centered Medical Home" Model of Primary Care in MTFs. Washington, DC, Office of the Secretary of Defense (Health Affairs), 2009.

2009

On July 9, Catherine Arnst of Business Week Magazine published a major feature article *"The Family Doctor: A Remedy for Health-Care Costs? How making primary care physicians the center of America's health system could ease the burden,*" featuring Dr. Paul Grundy and Dr. Peter Anderson.

2009

During 2009-2010, Dr. Peter Anderson collaborates with CTR Sean Lynch, CDR Kevin Dorrance and LCDR Sunny Ramchandani at Bethesda and learns how the *medical home* is shaping military medicine.

2009

In December, the Military Health System adopts the standard assessment process and accreditation of the independent, objective outside organization — NCQA.

2009

Multiple pilot projects for the *medical home* are in process and early findings begin to be published. As of December 31, 2009, there were at least 26 pilot projects involving *medical home*s with external payment reform being conducted in 18 states.

2009

TransforMED's Medical Home Implementation Quotient (IQ) version 2.0 is developed.

2009

In April, Dr. Anderson's practice becomes the first NCQA certified *medical home* in Virginia.

2010

Dr. Paul Grundy appears before the 7th Annual World Health Care Congress in April stating that "There is no system in the world that works without a robust base of primary care."

2010

URAC Patient Centered Health Care Home (PCHCH) Program Toolkit released.

2010

The Health Resources and Services Administration (HRSA) issues Program Assistance Letter (PAL) 2011-01 in November 2010 which describes HRSA's Patient-Centered Medical/Health Home (PCMHH) Initiative to support PCMH recognition for Section 330 funded organizations (medical care clinics).

2010

The Patient Protection and Affordable Care Act (PPACA), or the Affordable Care Act, is a United States federal statute signed into law.

2010

On June 10, Navy LCDR Sunny Ramchandani is named a White House Fellow, soon assigned to be the first Chief Medical Officer of the Federal Employee Health Benefit program where he rapidly integrates the *medical home* model.

2010

On September 8, an historic meeting is hosted by the PCPCC and sponsored by the Commonwealth Fund and Dartmouth Institute for Health Policy and Clinical Practice.

2010

In November *Family Team Care* began its part of the transformation of the U.S. Army's 21 new ambulatory care clinics.

2011

URAC announces PCMH auditor certification program as well as practice recognition program.

2011

The National Association of Community Health Centers (NACHC) launches its Patient Centered Medical Home Institute (PCMHI) and HRSA's Bureau of Primary Health Care (BPHC) announces the release of the Affordable Care Act supplemental grant opportunity for existing section 330 health centers to support the costs associated with enhancing systems and to become PCMHs.

2011

In September, LCDR Ramchandani leaves the Fellowship post and begins work on the next generation of the *medical home* model with CDR Kevin Dorrance and Dr. Paul Grundy, with San Diego as a pilot site.

2012

On June 28, The U.S. Supreme Court upholds the constitutionality of the health care reform act.

2012

The NCQA honors Dr. Paul Grundy with its 2012 Health Quality Award.

2013

Dr. Peter Anderson begins work on *The Familiar Physician*, a book designed as an urgent call to arms for patients and doctors, elected officials and health administrators in America to defend the future of primary care, embrace the *medical home* model, or be crushed by the changes ahead.

CHAPTER 9

TRANSFORMING MEDICAL OFFICES ONE EXAM ROOM AT A TIME

On-site Training Is What Works

Once more, back to Newport News and my medical practice, which is making record financial gains. I have doubled my daily caseload. I am going home on time, which greatly pleases my wife Laurie, and I am not finishing up records once I get there. I am seeing the patients who call in for an urgent appointment the same day they call. My patient satisfaction numbers go through the roof. My nursing staff is working at the top of their license and loving what they are doing. The quality of our care goes up by every measure. Once again I am receiving pleasure through the practice of medicine.

At the same time, the success we're experiencing is causing a stir.

Word of mouth spreads the news and I start receiving calls every day from health care executives and doctors asking to come see what we we're doing.

"You know you have to write a book about this," Laurie tells me one night at dinner.

"You know, some sort of guide for physicians across the country," she says. "Doctors who are up against the same problems you were. It would be a great way of giving back."

"I didn't do so well in English at UVA," I remind her. As a pre-med student writing and literature were never at the top of my list of academic passions. But Laurie stays with the idea. Eventually, I make a start on it and she cheers me on over the next year as I assemble everything we are learning in our practice through this thousand days of challenge and excitement.

"this has legs"

It takes over a year to finish the book, and I visit a good friend in the public affairs business. He studies it carefully.

"This has legs, Peter. This is important. You have to get his this out."

As I put together the final touches on what eventually takes the form of a handbook entitled, *"Liberating the Family Physician,"* I sense that the timing is right and I want to help my colleagues achieve what we are managing to do at my practice.

At the high end of my wish list, I am hoping that the handbook will create a wave of change across primary care in America. It contains all the details of *Family Team Care* that I could think of, all of the explanations for implementing our *inside the exam room* team care approach. I included the years of work we did in the review of symptoms to use as a "pre-flight checklist" in the exam room for every patient complaint. It would be easy from here, I am thinking. It's a very accurate and detailed map and all any practice has to do is follow it.

I sell hundreds of books to physicians and medical executives, absolutely certain that within six months, each of the doctors who used this handbook would be able to achieve what it had taken us years to perfect.

I personally called many of the doctors and executives who had purchased the book to get their feedback. What they told me was that the handbook itself was clear in its directions … but they didn't really make any of the major changes that were characteristic of my practice. They were so busy keeping their heads above water that true transformational change was simply out of reach.

This may not come as a surprise to anyone but most if not all physicians tend to be determined individuals who by training and probably natural inclination, set their eye on the prize and go for it. We are taught to be strong and, for the most part, independent practitioners of medicine. Yet that strength is also a potential downfall. For *Family Team Care* to be realized, the physician has to create, as the name infers, a sense of team. And building that team can't come only from a book.

DR. PETER ANDERSON AND
FAMILY TEAM CARE IN THE NEWS

Medical Economics, August 3, 2007 An effective way to use assistants—Training nurses and MAs to take histories and provide patient education boosts productivity, income, and quality of care

—By **Ken Terry**

"With primary care reimbursement steadily dropping, having assistants do more of the clinical spadework is a cost-effective option to consider. You'll need to know how to get started, how team-based care works, and what some experts say about it."

It involves looking at the world in a different light. It means changing from Superman or Superwoman to a team leader.

So to help doctors' offices bring the *Family Team Care* model to fruition, we produced a series of instructional DVD's with clear messages and high production values. Physicians bought them up in droves.

But that didn't work either. The many benefits of *Family Team Care* were just not coming into focus for the colleagues who had purchased these materials.

"It's like handing a drowning man a book on how to swim when what he really needs is for someone to either throw him a life jacket or better, come help him out of the water"

I realized then that transitioning to *inside the exam room* team care is such a fundamental change, such a major transformation, that it could not be accomplished with a book and DVD no matter how well produced or intended.

It's like handing a drowning person a book on how to swim when what he or she really needs is for someone to either throw a life jacket or better, come in the water and help.

Business Week Magazine

On July 9 of that year, Catherine Arnst of Business Week Magazine published a major feature article, *"The Family Doctor: A Remedy for Health-Care Costs? How making primary care physicians the center of America's health system could ease the burden."*

She visited our practice and wrote about the enormous differences she saw there and the news spread around the nation, strengthening both Dr. Grundy's crusade for the *medical home* and for our model, which strongly supports the *medical home* concept and the changing role of the primary care doctor.

Needless to say, the phones began to ring. One of the many visitors to our office is a medical doctor and a lieutenant colonel from the U.S. Army, LTC Martin Doperak, who has been sent to investigate if patient satisfaction and operational efficiencies within their ambulatory care centers could be improved with the *Family Team Care* model.

His last remark to me after a couple hours of watching our team work is, "When I get back to the Pentagon and tell them what I have seen, they are going to think I was high on drugs."

PART FOUR

Steady handoffs between civilian and military leadership rapidly advance the *medical home* movement

In the civilian medical world, we see a well-coordinated team emerge uniting everyone around the *medical home* as a way to deliver health care now and in the future.

In the Military Health System, another powerful team emerges into the light, gathering leadership around this bold, brilliant idea.

In almost perfect parallel to what took place in the civilian world, the military world sees a visionary leader prepare the strategy while another devotes his career to making it happen on the ground.

CHAPTER 10

THE MILITARY HEALTH SYSTEM EMBRACES THE *MEDICAL HOME*

*Dr. Paul Grundy and
Navy CDR Kevin Dorrance, MD
Take the Helm*

D r. Paul Grundy's influence on the health care system in America also extended to the leadership of the Military Health System with over 9.7 million beneficiaries.

As Dr. Grundy moves forward with the coalition of believers in the *medical home*, the acceptance of this innovative model starts to become more commonplace throughout medicine.

Just as the rest of the nation has been grappling with rising health care costs, the Military Health System is facing similar increases. Reasons include:

- An increase in over 400,000 beneficiaries since 2007
- Expansion of entitlements to include TRICARE for Life (which made TRICARE the second largest payor to Medicare for the over-65 beneficiaries) and coverage for military reservists, higher utilization rates of civilian providers and health care institutions (designated as the purchased care sector) for emergency and specialty care
- A 70% increase in active duty service members' outpatient purchased care, and medical inflation rate far in excess of the general inflation rate

- Patient satisfaction in military treatment facilities is a relatively flat at 77% while beneficiaries seen in the purchased care sector have reported a satisfaction rate of 87%

the enormous Military Health System needs re-tooling

Like the broken civilian medical system, the enormous Military Health System needs re-tooling and it would be hard to find someone to disagree with that pronouncement.

Most of the command is well aware of the powerful coalition being built by Dr. Paul Grundy, uniting the stakeholders in civilian medicine unlike any other initiative in history.

Navy Commander Kevin Dorrance, MD, FACP

Navy CDR Kevin A. Dorrance is currently Chief, Internal Medicine, and Assistant Deputy Commander, Medical Services, at Walter Reed National Military Medical Center Bethesda. As head of Internal Medicine, he adapts and implements the first Patient-Centered *Medical Home* in the Military Health System, where he now focuses on the future *Medical home 2.0* and population health management.

Deeply attracted to the *medical home* concept, CDR Dorrance attends the early meetings of the PCPCC with the late Dr. Paul Florentino, who becomes the leadership support CDR Dorrance needs to make the *medical home* a reality in the Navy and the basis for expansion throughout military medicine.

Commander Dorrance builds a *Medical Home* transformation team

He puts together a dynamic team that includes:
LCDR Dwight Hampton, RN
LCDR John McGlorthan, RN
CDR Patricia Miller
CTR Sean Lynch
LCDR Sunny Ramchandani

Lucille Ball and the Chocolate Factory

At Bethesda National Naval Medical Center, now Walter Reed, the biggest military hospital operation in the world, CDR Dorrance explains that he had been very dissatisfied with "our ability to impact the lives of our patients in any fundamental way, to truly improve their lives and reduce the burden of their, too numerous, chronic conditions."

He embraced the Chronic Care Model with several clinics and made a difference in the management of chronic illness.

But his frustration, which he relates to a famous 1950's era TV sitcom, continues.

"This vision of *Lucille Ball and the Chocolate Factory* TV skit on 'I Love Lucy' struck me as a great metaphor for what we were facing with the ever increasing burden of chronic disease and our inability to stem the tide," CDR Dorrance explains. The skit featured the comedienne working in a chaotic and poorly organized candy factory where she was quickly overwhelmed by the rapid assembly line of chocolates.

"The PCMH model was an eye opener for me and I decided that we needed to move away from individual diseases and organs and move to a holistic approach that leverages what we in primary care were really trained to do — manage a person's life not just their conditions," CDR Dorrance recalls.

"I found the current approach lacking the foundation of primary prevention and what I had been calling a move from health care to health and this became the focus as we built the model for the Military Health System, at the National Naval Medical Center," he adds.

As the civilian health care community gains momentum, the initial planning and testing of the PCMH within the world of military health began in 2007.

Lieutenant Commander Suneil "Sunny" Ramchandani, MD, FACP, MC USN

At Bethesda, CDR Dorrance taps LCDR Suneil "Sunny" Ramchandani, MC USN to help start up a full-scale effort to spearhead the change to the *medical home* model.

"I started taking vital notes literally on the back of a napkin just before a meeting of a larger group of Navy leadership in Portsmouth, VA one night in 2007," LCDR Ramchandani recalls.

a movement is born

CDR Dorrance pulled aside a group of Internists, taking advantage of the ability to have a core group of thought leaders together, courtesy of the annual Navy chapter of the American College of Physicians meeting.

"We met and put together the basic components our PCMH model with these individuals."

The moment that the *medical home* is really born for military medicine is at this brief meeting before the presentation. CDR Dorrance remembers it clearly.

He and LCDR Ramchandani were gathered with four other key medical officers and visionaries.

Present were:

CAPT William Shimeall, (Internal Medicine Residency Program Director)
MAJ Jeff LaRochelle Uniformed Services University and Assistant Program Director)
CDR Alaric Franzos (Interim Department Head of Internal Medicine)
LCDR Justin Harder (an Internal Medicine resident at that time, brought in to have a young perspective)

They thought about ways in which they could help not only the Navy's medical program, but also improve other parts of the Military Health System.

LCDR Ramchandani and CDR Dorrance knew that the military medical system had to adopt something far more than just a cosmetic fix. They had long discussions of the emerging civilian *medical home* model and the leadership exhibited by Dr. Paul Grundy in gathering the stakeholders together. Dr. Grundy's founding of the PCPCC helped pave the way for a smooth acceptance of their plan through the chain of command.

"Commander Dorrance and I became a very effective one-two punch, " Lt. Commander Ranchandani says.

"And Dr. Paul Grundy's contribution was huge."

"Commander Dorrance carried the message upward through the command structure while I operationalized the roll out for the Patient-Centered Medical Home for military medicine."

They created a ten-page plan. The precise and well coordinated effort they put into place "felt like the teamwork portrayed on bridge of the Enterprise in *Star Trek* with Captain Kirk and Spock," LCDR Ramchandani notes, explaining that CDR Dorrance provided the confident leadership of Captain Kirk.

I enjoy telling the story of how the *medical home* is created by the Military Health System. It reminds us of the power of passionate belief in your work.

It's the same level of passion we saw generated in the civilian sector with Dr. Sepúlveda, Dr. Grundy and everyone associated with the *medical home* movement.

Along with the passion of the participants, what's truly consistent in both the civilian and military experiences is the absolute commitment by the leadership. When you view the effort through the eyes of CDR Dorrance, LCDR Ramchandani or Dr. Sarita Mobley you see the same thing — they are "all in."

While the decisions and support to deploy the *medical home* model are somewhat easier in military medicine because of the more cohesive and uniform structure, the culture and the existing processes are just as challenging to change as in civilian medicine.

Dr. Sarita Mobley

CDR Dorrance selects Dr. Sarita Mobley, board-certified in family medicine, to drive the change needed in Navy medicine for the first *medical home*s. Being the first person in that particular role, CDR Dorrance says that while there were no pre-conceived notions regarding the approach, she still had to overcome certain tradition-related obstacles, carry out a considerable amount of team building and help people evolve toward a new way of thinking about primary care.

"Our trip to the Southcentral Foundation was very important to us as we planned and launched the *medical home*. They deserve great attribution for what they taught us and continue to teach others," CDR Dorrance recalls.

DR. PETER ANDERSON AND *FAMILY TEAM CARE* IN THE NEWS

Family Practice Management July—August 2008, *A New Approach to Making Your Doctor-Nurse Team More Productive. With proper training and delegation, your team can see more patients, deliver better care and feel more satisfied at work.* Peter Anderson, MD and Marc D. Halley, MBA

"From a business perspective, the success of a medical practice is driven by the revenue side of the income statement. Many medical groups have had to extend their hours and reduce the time they spend with patients to remain viable. These changes have sometimes strained patient relationships and have added to physicians' frustrations. The team care approach dramatically enhances a family physician's ability to see additional patients while improving quality of care."

Southcentral Foundation is an Alaska Native-owned, non-profit health care organization serving nearly 60,000 Alaska Native and American Indian people living in Anchorage, the Matanuska-Susitna Valley, and 60 rural villages. Their vision is an overall community that enjoys physical, mental, emotional and spiritual wellness; its mission is to work together with the Native Community to achieve this wellness through health and related services.

The organization has developed and implemented comprehensive health-related services to meet the changing needs of the Native Community, enhance culture and empower individuals and families to take charge of their lives.

The Southcentral Foundation continues to receive national acclaim for its unique organizational and health care system. The Nuka System of Care developed there was featured as a model for other health care organizations in the New York Times editorial, *"A Formula for Cutting Health Costs."* As part of a series of articles on Alaska Native and American Indian health and wellness, The Oregonian published the article, *"Alaska Native medical center a model for curbing costs, improving health."*

Dr. Mobley briefly described the observed Nuka model as an approach that included a strong focus on relationships, integrated patient care, same day access to primary care and a clearly defined role for patients in their own health care.

"Dr. Mobley's contribution at the clinical execution point should not be underestimated and was so very much appreciated by myself and the rest of the clinic," CDR Dorrance notes.

"We had a tremendous cultural hurdle to get over and without her we would not have succeeded. I still remember our numerous meetings going over draft after draft of SOP's and job objectives/roles and responsibilities. I will never forget the provider 'one problem per visit' discussions that seemed to crop up in many drafts."

I meet Dr. Sarita Mobley on one of my visits to Bethesda to see CDR Dorrance and his team. She is the ideal person to launch a *medical home* — positive and extremely focused from the very start, energetic and a true believer in this model of medicine. She is all about the patient.

CDR Dorrance is a wonderful mentor when it comes to a patient-centered model, she notes.

"Beneficiaries want to be seen quickly, by the same person, and they want to feel important. CDR Dorrance feels strongly about creating a nurturing environment so patients feel that their needs are the most important thing."

Dr. Mobley also pilots important architectural changes, altering the environment for team care with no private offices and a team-centric environment to improve communications and workflow.

Initially, moving people into workspaces designed to support team medicine was a challenge, Dr. Mobley recalls.

"There are a lot of apprehension and privacy concerns. But when we did it, the staff liked it. I can turn around and say to my RN or LPN, 'we need to do this' — within arms reach. Nurses love that too."

Dr. Mobley's journey through the military medical system reminds us that the *medical home* cannot be fully accomplished overnight. The medical team has to be brought together and that in itself requires a considerable effort. On-site training is vital, and it may take a while before the new platform begins to take hold. There's also the question of continuity because in the military environment, providers move around more than in civilian medicine.

Dr. Sarita Mobley serves three years at Bethesda and then serves with the VA, stimulating the *medical home* model there. Later still, she brings her skills and experience with the *medical home* to the Army.

She relates that they designed and deployed the group-based architectural office environment when she led the *inside the exam room* team care training and *medical home* development at Ft. Benning, Georgia, a few years later.

My *Family Team Care* training group had the honor of being part of that on-site training at Ft. Benning.

"I like the architectural changes that are part of the overall transition to team care. It's really not that important to have a private office. Ultimately, it's what works best for the patient that directs the physical set up," Dr. Mobley adds.

"Who knew that when I met Dr. Anderson when I was in Bethesda that I would find myself a short time later in Fort Benning at North Columbia *Medical Home*, training my team with Dr. Anderson's excellent training staff, using the Anderson model!"

I am gratified by her kind words. Her enthusiasm for the *medical home* and her commitment to it has helped immensely to encourage its development throughout the military.

Today, Dr. Sarita Mobley has opened a private practice, the Providence Family Medicine Clinic, in Lumpkin, Georgia near her home. She is shooting for certification as a level 3 *medical home* model, as designated by the National Committee for Quality Assurance (NCQA) — and you can bet she will get there.

Dr. Grundy influences military medicine

Commander Ramchandani meets Dr. Paul Grundy in person for the first time in the Spring of 2008, when they asked IBM for support in developing some IT tools for the Navy's *medical home* program.

"The *medical home* is a great innovation. Paul's contribution to our process was enormous," Commander Ramchandani notes.

CDR Dorrance calls Dr. Paul Grundy an essential resource at this time.

"We benefited from the basic model and used the national platform to get our senior leaders engaged. I invited Paul to our PCMH Summits in 2008 and 2010 and introduced him to senior Military Health System and Veterans Health Services leadership."

CDR Dorrance recalls how Dr. Grundy "took this and moved forward as a key voice spreading the PCMH message across the services and Veterans Health Administration."

"He gained a lot of respect and kept senior leaders fully engaged. I presented our early outcomes to the Navy DSG Rear Adm. Thomas R. Cullison and was invited to present to Military Health System leaders in late 2008. RADM Cullison became very engaged and made the PCMH a significant point of policy for Navy Medicine," CDR Dorrance explains.

And in 2008, the VA adopts the model for their eight million beneficiaries.

The United States Department of Veterans Affairs (VA) is a government-run military veteran benefit system with Cabinet-level status. It is the United States government's second largest department, after the Department of Defense. With a total budget of over $152.6 billion planned in 2014, VA employs nearly 280,000 people at hundreds of Veterans Affairs medical facilities, clinics, and benefits offices and is responsible for administering programs of veterans' benefits for veterans, their families, and survivors.

It is also in 2008 that the Patient-Centered Medical Home model is implemented at Edwards Air Force Base in California and Ellsworth Air Force Base in South Dakota.

THE MILITARY HEALTH SYSTEM CORE PRINCIPLES
OF THE *MEDICAL HOME*

It was necessary for military medicine to adapt the original seven principles of the "House of Primary Care" to fit military-unique policies and procedures.

Specifically, the core principles within the Military Health System are the following:

Personal physician is defined as a provider (i.e., physician, nurse practitioner, or physician assistant) who is assigned as the "Primary Care Manager by Name."

Physician-directed medical practice is a team of military or civilian health care professionals (i.e., physician, nurse practitioner, physician assistant, independent duty corpsman, medical technician, and support staff) under the leadership of a primary care physician as team leader.

Whole person orientation is the expectation of the active and retired military service members that all aspects of care will be comprehensively addressed for themselves and their family members.

Care is coordinated or integrated as an established part of the TRICARE medical benefit, and all military beneficiaries are entitled to comprehensive, coordinated, and accessible primary care.

Quality and safety are embraced by the MHS' evidenced-based model of care, which includes an evidence-driven medical benefit, an extensive Department of Defense/Veterans Affairs Clinical Practice Guidelines Program, comprehensive Health Care Effectiveness Data and Information Set (HEDIS) and ORYX reporting and monitoring, and a sophisticated patient safety program.

Enhanced access is formally established within the MHS by access standards for primary care including acute, routine, and wellness visits.

(Payment that recognizes added value is the principle that remains a challenge due to the nature of the MHS' federal funding and financial incentives related to pay-for-performance.)

Available at http://www.health.mil/libraries/HA_Policies_and_Guidelines/09-015.pdf.

While the health leaders within the military strive to move millions of people toward the *medical home* model my staff and I continue to improve our *Family Team Care* medicine project. At that point, our paths converge.

My first contact with the visionary military physicians is in February 2009 when CAPT Robert C. Marshall of the Bureau of Medicine and Surgery connected us, and invited them to hear me speak at the Maryland Academy of Family Medicine conference on the *medical home.*

sweeping action

During this period both CMDR Dorrance and LCDR Ramchandani keynoted major events at the Patient-Centered Primary Care Collaborative. At that point, the sharing began in earnest between the military and civilian health care systems.

In 2009-2010, I travel to Bethesda to attend fact-finding meetings as they began to shape their approach to the military *medical home.* Working with CDR Dorrance, LCDR Ramchandni and CTR Sean Lynch to enlighten them as to the shape of the PCMH in civilian medicine, there again is Dr. Paul Grundy connecting people and ideas and championing the *medical home.*

On April 2, 2009, CDR Dorrance sends me correspondence that was very much appreciated. It comes at a time I need some encouragement. It's growing more and more frustrating and difficult to try to keep my full time practice and continue to maintain an active national speaking schedule.

"We had a wonderful time talking with you. It was great hearing your story and learning what it is like for our civilian colleagues. What you have done in the environment you work in is no less than remarkable! We are very interested in moving this forward and hopefully creating a hybrid model that may be more sustainable for the overall future of medicine in the U.S."

Meanwhile, LCDR Ramchandani recalls, Dr. Paul Grundy is "beating the drum, pushing the ball forward." He notes "There wasn't anybody as active in the field as Paul."

When you consider the scope of the Military Health System, you have to remember that it includes active duty, reservists, retirees and their dependents to age 21. Twenty-year retirees get medical care in the Military Health System, as do their dependents.

"So there are a lot of kids and a lot of older people. As a result, we have the same problems and issues as the general population of America," LCDR Ramchandani notes.

In September 2009, the Office of the Assistant Secretary of Defense (Health Affairs) directed *medical home* implementation throughout the Military Health System. This action establishes the Patient-Centered Medical Home as the foundation for refocusing the MHS' primary health care delivery model within the MHS. Primary care specialties include Family Medicine, Internal Medicine, Pediatrics, Undersea Medicine, and Flight Medicine.

After returning from a year-long deployment to Afghanistan in 2010, LCDR Sunny Ramchandani turned his thoughts to what he wanted to do next. He had served as a staff internist at the National Naval Medical Center (Bethesda), and had really enjoyed being part of the team that helped launch the Navy's *Medical Home Port* program. As he talked with his close associate CDR Dorrance, they thought about ways in which they could help improve other parts of the health care system.

"We both thought, in addition to the *medical home*, there were some very innovative ideas that we could help promote throughout the Military Health System," Ramchandani said.

"CDR Dorrance really stressed the importance of how we needed to figure out ways in which we could promote *health* instead of *health care*."

DR. PETER ANDERSON AND
FAMILY TEAM CARE IN THE NEWS

Business Week, July 6, 2009, The Family Doctor — A Remedy for Health-Care Costs? How making primary-care physician the center of America's health system could ease the burden.

—By **Catherine Arnst**

"Unlike most primary-care doctors, Anderson and his team take ample time to counsel patients, guide them through lifestyle changes, and monitor chronic conditions with frequent check-ups. He has helped patients avoid heart attacks, diabetes and unnecessary surgeries by focusing on prevention and disease monitoring. He does all this while seeing 30 to 35 patients a day, compared with 20 to 25 for most practices. 'This is what I always wanted to do," says the 56-year-old Anderson, who converted to a *medical home* five years ago. "I'm seeing far more patients and delivering the best care I've ever done."

CHAPTER 11

BACK TO MY STORY

With a Thriving Practice, I Quit to Help the U.S. Army

So, following the directive for the entire Military Health System to move out smartly to the *medical home* model, the U.S. Army begins their implementation of the Patient-Centered Medical Home.

Once again, the work my staff and I have been doing becomes part of the larger story.

The United States Army begins discussions with me through Dr. Tim Caffrey and LTC Brad Lieurance on a national assignment to convert each of their 21 ambulatory clinics of the pilot program into the *Family Team Care* model.

We discussed the goals of the Army and my sense that the handbook I produced and the DVDs that followed aren't sufficient to create the needed transformation is confirmed once again. On-site training is the only way to bring about the change.

I am elated when these two commanders agreed and set into motion what turns out to be a success story on a number of different levels. I know *Family Team Care* is incredibly effective, but now the Army is a believer — it took me awhile to fully realize all this had really happened and now, someone expected the whole thing to work out in a different setting.

Throughout this process, I felt the behind the scenes support of Dr. Paul Grundy.

On one hand I think I should feel a bit intimidated and even frightened by the scope of all this. It means, at the very least, a major change in my life. Because this project is such an important effort for the Army — and an overall $65 million expenditure —I am told that the Surgeon General of the Army thought about and discussed this initiative on a daily basis. Even with all this attention, though, there really isn't any fear. We have seen our model work and work well over the course of seven years and we know it's the right approach for primary care. Equally important, it's a better way to serve patients.

This next step with the Army also had the potential to change the culture of medicine on a very large scale. As it turns out, this Community Based Primary Care Clinic pilot project is one of the most extensive change experiments in medicine from the perspective of people reached, and these two commanders asked us to be part of it.

The U.S. Army's MEDCOM currently manages a $12.8 billion budget and cares for more than 1.8 million beneficiaries — active-duty members of all services, retirees and their family members.

So late in that year, we launched our *Family Team Care* training as part of the *medical home* transformation for the U.S. Army's 21 new clinics. At that point I would, once again, have the pleasure of working with the remarkable Dr. Sarita Mobley when our team did the on-site training at Ft. Benning.

It is at this moment, that I have to make one of the most difficult decisions of my life and certainly the most difficult of my career as a physician. With regards to my practice, I had just righted the ship. The *inside the exam room* team care model is working smoothly and the experience is better than ever for staff, patients and families. I am getting home on time and feeling more fulfilled in my life and my work.

But there is a decision to be made. I suppose if it were easy, it wouldn't be much of a decision. What I have come to understand in these past few months is that I cannot effectively carry out the Army contract and practice medicine at the same time. I simply can't "do" and "teach" simultaneously.

The decision comes down to leaving the work that I love, leaving the patients I've cared for, in some cases for over 20 years, to pursue a different direction.

I took a lot of long walks with Laurie. I talked with my nurses, my friends and my children.

"Ultimately, it was Dr. Paul Grundy who helped me make up my mind. His continuous call for a full-scale emphasis on the physician-patient relationship is made with a passion I have never quite seen before. And it helps me realize that in my own desire to strengthen that very special relationship I can reach more people through training than through my own practice.

"I am hoping to help Dr. Paul Grundy and his colleagues change the trajectory of primary care in America"

Leaving my practice in 2011 was tough to say the least. I never imagined how hard it would be to say good-bye to my patients. On the more positive side I didn't have to say good-bye to my nurses. They came with me, becoming professional trainers for *Family Team Care*.

I am hoping to help Dr. Paul Grundy and his colleagues change the trajectory of primary care in America. Anything less than this goal would be a disservice to the work I left behind and the love I have for being a doctor.

During the transition I receive heartwarming well wishes from many of my patients. One of the most memorable comes from Bob and Tammy Dessoffy, a couple who had relied on the trust and bond we had developed together over two decades.

After I announced my retirement, they said to me "You know, your office was the most amazing place. It was calm, almost reverent, joyful, relaxing. We used to love just being there. We will miss you so much."

As I move into this new role, this new world, really, I encounter a considerable amount of skepticism. And I understand why. Physicians all over America have been sold a bill of goods for years about remedies that will cure all the ills of the medical mess we find ourselves in. But shortly after we show up and enter their office to begin training, the skepticism transforms to hope.

The delivery of primary care at this moment looks essentially the same as it did 50 years ago. There are new diagnostic procedures, new treatments, new technologies, but the basic approach has altered very little. With the rest of health care changing so dramatically is there any wonder that primary care is struggling to keep up? The foundation of medicine in America is still the primary care provider, including internal medicine, family practice, osteopathic medicine and pediatrics. The front line of health care remains the same. But it is a front line that has weakened.

My contribution now to strengthening it is to do training on-site, to train the team in the office, and be a constant resource and coach with follow-ups from the *Family Team Care* nurse counselors. Equally important, my contribution now that I've left my own practice is to help other physicians believe that the *inside the exam room* team care medicine model will work for their practice.

In the process, the physicians and their staff see immediately that not only are we sure the new approach will improve their ability to practice medicine but that we take considerable pleasure in helping to make it happen.

I couldn't have made this change in my career without believing in the outcomes.

In his presentations across the country, Dr. Grundy continually reminds his audiences that elements of the current health care system are flawed.

"We tried it. We experimented with it. For thirty years and longer in this country, it's failed us. It's failed our health plan partners, it's failed our primary care doctors, it's failed our corporations, and it's failed our patients. It's failed all of us."

That's why I was sure, and remain so, that we had to do something different.

CHAPTER 12

BRINGING THE
MEDICAL HOME
TO FEDERAL EMPLOYEES
LCDR Ramchadani Helps Harness
the Power of the Federal Government

B ack in the U.S. Navy, LCDR Ramchandani has many soul-searching conversations with CDR Dorrance on the future of military medicine. Then an old Naval Academy friend suggested he apply for the White House Fellowship program.

Founded in 1964, the Fellowship allows young leaders to spend one year working in the offices of Cabinet Secretaries, Deputy Secretaries, and other high level Executive Branch officials.

Previous fellows include former Labor Secretary Elaine Chao, General Colin Powell, Governor Samuel Brownback, CNN Medical Correspondent Dr. Sanjay Gupta, writer Doris Kearns Goodwin, and Univision President Cesar Conde.

LCDR Ramchandani began the arduous application process, which required ten essays and multiple recommendation letters. After the entire process was complete, he had passed through 24 different interview panels; a few of these panelists included Tom Brokaw, General Wesley Clark (ret.), former Senator Thomas Daschle, and former Senator Paul Sarbanes.

In June 2010, he finally received the call to be the first Navy physician to ever be selected to the program.

"use the might of the federal government to promote the *medical home*"

LCDR Ramchandani was assigned to be the first Chief Medical Officer of the Federal Employee Health Benefit Program, which has an annual budget of $43 billion, serves 8 million beneficiaries and contains over 200 health care plans.

"At this point, we pushed hard on how to take the federal health benefit program and use the might of the federal government to promote the *medical home*."

And all that hard pushing paid off. By 2011, LCDR Ramchandani has been instrumental in extending the *medical home* model to all federal employees and their families.

"So if you tally up the impact of Dr. Paul Grundy on federal health care, you add 9 million military, 8 million VA beneficiaries and another 8 million federal employees, you have roughly 25 million people — that's a lot of folks in the system and Dr. Paul Grundy has played a big role in their medical future."

"There's are quite a few entities in the military health care system moving forward right now. We are "all in" on the *medical home*," LCDR Ramchandani concludes.

CHAPTER 13

SETTING STRONG STANDARDS FOR THE *MEDICAL HOME*

NCQA Takes the Lead

D espite the perfect storm hurtling towards primary care, the *medical home* concept is succeeding, even in a divisive political environment. What has helped make the difference is the leadership of IBM, the steady hand of the NCQA and a growing willingness by primary care physicians to change the way they practice.

The National Committee for Quality Assurance (NCQA) is an independent 501(c)(3) non-profit organization in the United States designed to improve health care quality.

It was established in 1990 with support from the Robert Wood Johnson Foundation. NCQA manages voluntary accreditation programs for individual physicians, health plans and medical groups.

"...holding a high standard"

The NCQA's definition of the Patient-Centered *Medical Home* is "a model of care that strengthens the clinician-patient relationship by replacing episodic care with coordinated care and a long-term healing relationship. Each patient has a relationship with a primary care clinician who leads a team that takes collective responsibility for patient care, providing for the patient's needs and arranging for appropriate care with other qualified clinicians. The *medical home* is intended to result in more personalized, coordinated, effective and efficient care."

With this well regarded organization holding a high standard for American health care delivery, and Dr. Paul Grundy helping to pull people together, I believe the *medical home* model, and hence the new health reform it helps support, will continue to exert a very positive influence on the health of populations and individuals.

In December 2009, the Military Health System adopts the NCQA's standard assessment process and accreditation measures.

NCQA manages voluntary accreditation programs for individual physicians, health plans, and medical groups. Health plans seek accreditation measure performance through the administration and submission of the Healthcare Effectiveness Data and Information Set (HEDIS) Consumer Assessment of Healthcare Providers and Systems (CAHPS) survey.

NCQA standards describe clear and specific criteria. The program gives practices information about organizing care around patients, working in teams and coordinating and tracking care over time. The NCQA Patient-Centered Medical Home standards strengthen and add to the issues addressed by NCQA's original program.

There are six PCMH 2011 standards, including six must-pass elements, which can result in one of three levels of recognition. Practices seeking PCMH complete a Web-based data collection tool and provide documentation that validates responses. The three-tiered recognition of NCQA allows physicians to make incremental progress over time toward comprehensive *medical home* services.

In recognition of his tireless efforts on behalf of the *medical home*, the NCQA honored Dr. Grundy with its 2012 Health Quality Award, a tribute based on the premise that "every good idea needs a visionary champion to sustain it in its early days until the concept catches on. For the delivery system innovation known as the Patient-Centered Medical Home, that champion is Paul Grundy of IBM."

Merck's Robert Dribbon

Speaking at the awards ceremony is Robert Dribbon, Director of Health Care System Strategy for Merck, who serves as Executive Committee Liaison for the PCPCC's Executive Committee.

"When Paul began his work on the Patient-Centered Medical Home, it was the mid 2000's. The *medical home* concept was not new. But what Paul did was to really take it under his wing and nurture it, which is why he is often called "the Godfather of the *Medical Home*."

"At the time, Paul saw the need for a leader, someone who could inspire stakeholders from across the system, bring them together, and rally around the Patient-Centered Medical Home concept," Robert Dribbon said.

"one thousand organizations"

"Paul shaped the PCPCC which is an organization now about five years in existence that has over one thousand organizations as members representing virtually all parts of the health care system."

"Paul has demonstrated time and time again by stepping up, taking the lead and inspiring us to always remember and place the patient at the center of everything we do," Robert Dribbon concludes.

The ACA health reform doesn't directly change how doctors practice medicine, but it does dramatically realign the business of medicine by driving virtually all of health care into an Accountable Care Organization. Ultimately, it is the payment reform of the Affordable Care Act that will restructure health care in America.

In very basic terms, the Accountable Care Organization model mandates that hospitals, emergency rooms and primary care providers work together. Primary care providers won't lose their private practices, but will face a strong value proposition to rethink the way those offices operate in cooperation with other providers.

"Providers are going to be accountable," Dr. Paul Grundy offers to the *2012 Innovations in Health Care Awards* event, at which he is being honored by Blue Cross and Blue Shield of North Dakota.

"While driving to speak to a group at a large east coast academic medical center, I passed a billboard that said something like, 'We deliver the absolute best heart surgery in the state' ."

"That's not the sign I want to see. I want to see a sign that says we deliver the best primary care with doctors you know and trust who are members of a patient-centered team."

There are places in this country right now that already seeing significant declines in surgeries because someone has the discipline to manage a population, to do blood pressure monitoring, aspirin therapy and cholesterol control, he concludes.

> "we cannot have accountable care
> without the *medical home* model"
> **— Dr. Paul Grundy**

We had a lot of people betting against us when we were developing *Family Team Care*. So many doctors have given up.

The viability of America's health system hinges on the ability of primary care providers to absorb not only 30-40 million new patients, but a huge increase in visits by existing patients who should have been seeing a primary care physician in the first place rather than going to a specialist or emergency room. Again, their willingness to change how they are organized is key to the survival of primary care.

**THE PATIENT-CENTERED PRIMARY CARE
COLLABORATIVE
RAPID EVOLUTION**

Today, the PCPCC's 1,000 members represent a diverse group of *medical home* advocates and stakeholders across the continuum of care, including employers, health professionals and clinicians, health plans, technology and pharmaceutical firms, policy makers, and consumer advocacy groups.

For more information about the PCPCC visit www. pcpcc.net

CHAPTER 14

A LOOK AT
MEDICAL HOME 2.0
Taking the First Step

CDR Kevin Dorrance at Walter Reed continues his exploration into the next level of care. Just as he carried the banner for the *medical home* in the Navy and Military Health System, now he focuses his energy on the next iteration.

"How do you make it a much more effective world?"

"health doesn't occur in a health care setting"

"We are examining proven benefits. I helped build a model that merges these two worlds," he says, "and it's exciting to see what health care will look like in the future."

He calls this vision of the future *Medical home 2.0*. He recently held a major *PCMH 2.0* Summit, attended by stakeholders from throughout the military and governmental agencies.

"Health doesn't occur in a health care setting," CDR Dorrance says.

"We are a nation struggling with a rising rate of preventable medical conditions. The solution has very little to do with what we traditionally think of as our health care system. We truly have an amazing health care system if you have a catastrophic condition or a traumatic event."

"Where we struggle," CDR Dorrance notes, "is in the production of health and well-being."

"The vast majority of our health care dollars are misdirected into the pharmaceutical industry and unnecessary testing that has little added value. We need a new strategy, one that understands that the real problem is lifestyle and poor health behaviors. The PCMH model provides the foundation by leveraging Behavioral Economic theories to create primary prevention programs we can move toward *PCMH 2.0*."

the San Diego project

LCDR Ramchandani leaves the Fellowship in September 2011 and begins collaborating again with Dr. Paul Grundy and with CDR Dorrance in designing the next generation of the *medical home* model. He is assigned to San Diego and given the innovative assignment to be a part of the pilot projects of *Medical home 2.0*.

Now, as the Medical Director for Healthcare Business at Naval Medical Center San Diego, LCDR Ramchandani is using what he learned in the Fellowship and Bethesda to implement an "Integrated Health Community" — a population health initiative designed to improve the health of all Navy beneficiaries in San Diego County.

With this assignment, his heart still lies with internal medicine, with primary care.

His collaborator on this initiative? Dr. Paul Grundy.

LCDR Ramchandani has a *Medical home 2.0.* seven-year plan for the San Diego, CA community.

moving from health care to health

His close associate CDR Kevin Dorrance continues to focus on the *medical home* implementation at his command in Walter Reed National Military Medical Center — pushing the envelope to integrate mind-body medicine and new IT tools into the military delivery of health care, with 30,000 enrolled in a pilot there.

"For the first time," CDR Dorrance notes, "we have full-time team members whose total focus is to move enrollees toward well being."

Dr. Grundy and many other innovative leaders see the creation of an integrated health community as the next step.

"Paul began working with us on this "final frontier" in August of 2011," Commander Ramchandani notes.

"I love this because we are addressing aggressively how we can make people healthier, not just delivering health care when you're sick. And we know that in order to do this, we must be part of the community lifestyle, fully integrated into what people do on a daily basis."

LCDR Ramchandani began the implementation of this cutting edge Military Health System initiative in November 2012. They have chosen the community of San Diego because of its extensive, existing military presence.

"San Diego has over 3.1 million people. It's the eighth largest city in America. Over $24 billion is spent in San Diego County every year on health care and 20 percent of that is paid for by the Department of Defense," LCDR Ramchandani notes.

Even more significantly, San Diego is a microcosm of the entire population of America as a whole. The disease incident rates, age of the population and other metrics line up almost perfectly with national averages.

"We are beginning our efforts with 'hotspotting', identifying who is costing the health care system the most and starting to work on these specific patients with a *medical home* model. The team is also taking a full inventory of community, social and health services. They are studying the $1 billion that San Diego spends on quality of life infrastructure, community and recreational resources, seeking ways to integrate the *medical home* model into those resources.

Years three through six will bring in very progressive incentives for health care services, community services as well as individual beneficiaries.

"as patients — we don't want health care, we want health"

LCDR Ramchandani says that "America is spending 17% of its GDP on health care and we still don't give people what they want.

"As patients, as consumers, we don't want health care, we want health. The spending is completely distorted. If we invest in community building, and integrate with the community, we can make better health a part of people's lives."

"As a doctor, I want there to be a new wave of pushing the idea of health. I want to be able to write a prescription for a gym, or for yoga…for actions that will help my patients achieve health," he notes.

Year 7 and onward is where LCDR Ramchandani sees cultural transformation from " health care" to "health" showing long-term measurable improvements.

"If you really want to affect population health, you must integrate with the community." Yet, the reason we have not done this so far is that there is no visible return on investment. Few incentives are in place. We know we can become a lot more efficient.

In his 2013 presentation to community groups in San Diego, LCDR Ramchandani underscores the importance of *Medical home 2.0* for the future.

"In an era of economic austerity, there is a direct tie of health to our financial solvency as a nation."

CHAPTER 15

EMPOWERING
THE PATIENT

The Third Leg of the Stool

U
sing the three-legged stool analogy, Dr. Paul Grundy believes that the importance of creating incentives for consumers to make good choices, such as taking medications as prescribed or having a *medical home* provider, is the third leg.

The first two legs of the stool, which we've already looked at, are the transformation of medical practices to the *medical home* model of care, and payment reform to reward managing a patient population and delivering better access and service.

"The third leg of the stool is how you engage and empower the consumer," Dr. Grundy notes, "and that involves the science of insurance design and incentives — blending wise benefit structure into health plans — and this approach has been in close development since we began the PCPCC."

Dr. Grundy explains that the current insurance model is so outdated and inefficient that it's like being told to go buy car with this admonition: No matter which model you buy, all you'll have to pay is a $20 out of pocket fee. What would happen? You'd see quite a few BMW's rolling off the lot not to mention some Rolls Royces and Maserati Gran Turisimos.

Dr. Grundy adds that under this scenario, no worries if you don't change the oil, stay current with the scheduled maintenance or keep the tires inflated

155

properly. If there's a problem, just get another new car. After all, it only takes that $20 co-pay.

Dr. Mark Fendrick

"In 2006, at that very first gathering of employers and primary care physicians, I was told by Andrew Webber at the National Business Coalition on Health that A. Mark Fendrick, MD, working at the University of Michigan, was helping to develop a better approach to incentivizing consumers to achieve better health."

"I called Dr. Fendrick that week. Mark called it value-based insurance design (V-BID) and was developing and testing theories regarding access to services and insurance product design."

"In my first conversation he told me they believed 'value' should be assessed by the benefit a patient would receive from the service delivered. This emphasis on patient-centered outcomes was a welcome deviation from the usual conversation about costs.

"I asked him if he was saying that if effective primary care adds real value, should it then be designed into the benefit package at no charge to employees; should it be available free?"

Dr. Fendrick considered the question and noted that such an approach would represent both a commitment and a truly robust approach to primary care.

remove the barriers

"He said that by removing financial and non-financial barriers to primary care, it adds real value. It should be free and made very, very easy to get. And maybe even create rewards if the consumers follow their therapy," Dr. Grundy notes.

"So, I added that in a perfect world, what you really want is for patients to take their chronic disease medication, which should be at zero cost to the patient, and possibly even involve a reward system as well," Dr. Grundy recalls.

Dr. Mark Fendrick, even at a time when the current direction of health care reform was not fully anticipated, was dedicated to changing the conversation from how *much* — to how *well* — we were spending our health care dollars.

So his "value-based" concept of patient cost-sharing abandons the archaic idea of "one-size-fits-all" to one that is "clinically-nuanced." This nuance recognizes that (1) medical services differ in the benefit provided; and (2) the clinical benefit derived from a specific service depends on the patient using it, as well as when, where and by whom the service is provided. Accordingly, V-BID plans reduce financial barriers to evidence-based services and high-performing providers (carrots) and/or impose disincentives to discourage use of low-value services and providers (sticks).

I clearly recognize this concept from three decades of experience in family medicine. When patients take their medication properly for diabetes or high blood pressure, they not only stay healthier and happier, the overall cost of their care drops significantly.

A V-BID approach can address contradictions in our health care system by aligning incentives and establishing synergistic tools that produce desired behaviors and outcomes. Obviously, aligning incentives for consumers and providers is essential for the Patient-Centered Medical Home environment to be effective.

"At the time of our initial conversation, I was thrilled that Dr. Fendrick was already shaping the third leg of the stool, and we became partners in the collaborative," Dr. Grundy adds.

A. Mark Fendrick, MD is currently a Professor at the University of Michigan, Department of Internal Medicine and Health Management and Policy, and Director of the Center for Value-Based Insurance Design.

The ongoing study and results of years of analysis are reported in a white paper recently published by the PCPCC and the National Business Coalition on Health which outlines the effects of Value-Based Insurance Design at pioneering organizations such as Geisinger Health System, IBM, the State of Maine, Whirlpool, RoyOMartin Lumber, a large Louisiana-based forestry products firm, and others.

The study, co-written with Bruce Sherman, MD, and Dennis White, clearly shows that V-BID and the Patient-Centered Medical Home go hand-in-hand, delivery and demand, simultaneously changing provider and patient behaviors.

As part of the need to create a more efficient system, the white paper notes that a PriceWaterHouseCoopers examination estimates that $1.2 trillion per year in health care costs (almost half) is waste.

Value-Based Insurance Design layers on incentives to steer individuals to high-value practices as well as appropriate treatment and preventive care behavior objectives. In its most basic form, V-BID employer-driven benefit strategies provide incentives for higher value health care services while simultaneously reducing lower value health care expenditures.

For example, research indicates that sixty percent of chronically ill patients have poor adherence to treatment plans and ongoing care management. In these cases, reductions in co-payments for the treatment of asthma, diabetes and heart disease were offset by the reduced use of non-drug services. The end result was no net increase in medical expenses with improved outcomes for patients.

Other research demonstrates that the use of mammography decreases when the patient co-pay increases. Again, we see that higher co-pays function as a barrier to good preventive care.

We caught up with Dr. Fendrick while preparing The *Familiar Physician*, and he offered the following thoughts:

"There is nothing like an intuitive idea that you can get passionate about," he said, referring to his seminal work on value-based insurance design.

"PCMH and V-BID go hand-in-glove in aligning incentives on the delivery and demand sides to improve health care quality."

"The sum is greater than the parts," Dr. Fendrick notes.

But just as employers have played an important role in embracing the *medical home* model, Dr. Fendrick believes that these same employers will be essential in improving population health through the benefit design they make available to their employees.

Dr. Grundy reflected that the coming designs of health plans bring him back to his very first conversation he had with Dr. Doug Henley. He told Dr. Henley that IBM and other employers would like to buy care of greater value. They wanted, in the most basic terms, proactive primary care.

"I clearly remember what Dr. Henley said to me, Dr. Grundy recalls. Doug said 'bless your heart' ."

"He said that we would like you to start reimbursing us for that kind of care management and stop covering low value episodes of care."

"What I believed then and continue to believe now, Dr. Grundy added, "is that the work of Dr. Mark Fendrick and his team is vital in helping America re-

"*Medical home* shows great promise; however, even if the cultural transition is handled well, it cannot be assumed that it will remain an unchallenged norm. Rather, a new culture is a dynamic and fragile entity that has to be supported, led, and invigorated on a regular basis."

"The key period of establishing a new culture is not at the onset of transformation, when behaviors, procedures, and policies need to be changed. Rather, the key alterations in norms and shared values come at the end of the transformational process, when new behavioral patterns need to become normative and employees need to be strengthened against backsliding into old, nonproductive ways. Implementing PCMH brings with it remarkable new challenges and dramatic change in the culture of care."

Protecting the Culture of a Patient-Centered Medical Home

CDR Kevin A. Dorrance, MC USN;
LCDR Suneil Ramchandani, MC USN;
MAJ Jeff LaRochelle, MC USA;
Fred Mael, PhD;
Sean Lynch, BS;
Paul Grundy, MD,
Military Medicine, Volume 178, Issue 2, pages 153-158.

shape health care delivery. It's truly the third leg of the stool, and we could not get everything else to work without this value-based design."

PART FIVE:

The work continues to preserve
The *Familiar Physician*

Dr. Grundy is once again crisscrossing America — circling back to many of the hundreds of communities he has visited over these years, to remind the medical community of the basic reasons we have moved in this direction and to keep everyone up-to-date on the latest successes.

"Driving the change to the *medical home* model are three major factors.

First — unsustainable cost," he notes. He elaborates on how poorly America does in comparison with other developed nations when it comes to health care expenditures and return on investment.

"Second — for the first time, we have data, detailed information, from which we can re-design health care delivery." He mentions that we have pilot programs out there in a number of states and that we have been gathering data for years. "We know what things cost now and we can see the difference in communities across America."

"Third — we have an innovation imperative. My adult kids, the next generation, will not accept things as they are. Young people want answers," Dr. Grundy explains.

CHAPTER 16

THE *MEDICAL HOME* MODEL IS BRINGING SOMETHING SPECIAL

Success in Vermont

N ow as I speak to groups around the country, I remind my colleagues that in the last decade we have drifted away from where we need to be. Because there is limited access to our primary doctor, urgent care centers are thriving with episodic care. Emergency rooms are filled with primary care patients and patients who are seeing their doctors are disgruntled with long waits in the midst of equally frustrated office staff.

Primary care doctors are awakening to the need to re-engineer how they practice and embrace the concept of the *Familiar Physician.*

"I'm a glass half full kind of guy," says Dr. Doug Henley of AAFP, an organization representing over 110,600 physicians.

"I am excited about what we have achieved but there is more work to be done.

"There is still important work to do but we'll get it right," Dr. Henley suggests.

"As Sir Winston Churchill once said 'you can always count on Americans to do the right thing — after they've tried everything else first.' "

Dr. Henley acknowledges that we have not yet "nailed the full notion of patient-centered instead of provider-centered" care.

"Woefully, he notes, "our health care is currently designed in a uniquely American way — to cost a lot of money, to make some people a lot of money, and yet we have not delivered on the promise of improved quality and cost efficiency in health care to the American people."

pioneering the *medical home* model

Yet wonderful progress is being made by many states — the Department of Defense, the VA, our nation's community health centers, Maryland, Michigan, Rhode Island, Maine and Vermont all have made great strides in pioneering the *medical home* model.

Compelling evidence that this new system will be effective is supported by the state of Vermont, which began a bold experiment called the Vermont *Blueprint for Health*. Launched by Gov. Jim Douglas in 2003, *Blueprint* began to gain traction in 2007 and is now generating some nationwide attention as a maturing success story fundamentally based on the Patient-Centered Medical Home model. It also has a strong mental health component.

available when needed

Dr. Paul Grundy, along with news magazines and medical journals, is pointing to this impressive initiative, which brings all insurers and providers together, for a preview of what medical care could look like at the end of the day.

"Look at what we're doing in Vermont," Dr. Grundy urges.

At the heart of the Vermont *Blueprint* are:

- Patients — individual and unique care with the personal attention and support they need to take charge of their own health
- Doctors and their health care teams — available when needed
- Community Health Teams that connect patients to resources beyond the doctor's office
- Workshops and support groups that help patients reach their own goals
- Prevention and wellness services
- Computerized health records
- Free support services

Community Health Team members work hand in hand with patients, doctors and their staff to help patients set goals and receive the education and tools they need to improve their health. Focused on both treatment and prevention, these teams include nurses and specialists in nutrition, exercise, counseling, and more. Their focus is to help patients:

- Eat healthier
- Become more physically active
- Quit smoking
- Understand their treatment plan
- Manage their medications
- Manage their health condition
- Connect with local resources such as transportation services, and community walking paths
- Talk to someone about the challenges that can get in the way of leading a healthier life
- Receive care coordination from a hospital stay back to a primary care doctor
- Prevent small problems from becoming big ones

Vermont's Craig A. Jones, MD

The *2012 Vermont Blueprint for Health Annual Report*, demonstrates significant drops in hospitalization rates and costs per person for health care.

Dr. Craig A. Jones, Executive Director of *Blueprint for Health* has been with this unique project since 2007. He too, has seen the impact of the championing of the Patient-Centered Medical Home by Dr. Paul Grundy.

"We began *Blueprint* when Paul was beginning to make a footprint across the country," Dr. Jones notes.

"Paul helped make it come alive by growing the interest of the nation's health care leaders in the importance of the Vermont project. Without his influence, we might not have been able to get it all together. He can move people — walk into a room and organize everyone around a common vision. In his spectacular way, Dr. Paul Grundy quietly helped bring everyone together."

AMERICA'S CHAMPIONS OF PRIMARY CARE
"Paul hit the right moment, bringing long-term institutional organizations together who were historically competitors — and they found a calling much bigger than the issues."

— Katherine Herring Capps, President, Health2 Resources.

Dr. Grundy's many presentations include supporting data, demonstrating each of his points clearly and gently. His data now reflects the successes seen in the many pilot programs going on across the nation.

He underscores that the new alignment of incentives cannot be underestimated. Finance is finally going to be aligned with quality. For decades, we have actually been rewarding sickness instead.

It is both sad and personally unsatisfying for me to recall that the sicker my patients were, the more money I made. I am very gratified to be a part of a movement that is relegating that unsustainable payment model to history.

Katie Capps

Katie Capps of Health2Resources who guided the communications campaign to create and grow the Patient-Centered Primary Care Collaborative, and help rally American health care on the *medical home* in the process, sums up Paul Grundy's inspirational presence.

"Paul can encounter a difficult situation in a crowded room and turn it into an opportunity for everyone," she notes.

"There's a special Code with these folks," Katie Capps, continues. "Meetings are set with just a phone call and everyone comes. There is a sense of urgency, the feeling that if we don't do this now, it will be a disaster."

Bert Miuccio

Bert Miuccio of TransforMed echoes that sentiment.

"Today, it's amazing to go to a meeting, and this has happened several times, where a speaker pauses in the presentation and asks if the audience knows of Dr. Paul Grundy and his work. This happened at the 2013 Texas Health Home Summit and 80 percent of the audience raised their hands."

"And when his name is mentioned, smiles break out," Bert Miuccio notes.

"Paul's work has not come without personal sacrifice," Katie Capps adds.

"His constant travel throughout the country and world to stay well attuned to the Patient-Centered Medical Home Pilot Projects in this country, as well as his favored *medical home* nations abroad has created many sacrifices caused by being away from home," she adds.

As a silent testament to his extensive travel, Paul Grundy's passport has been handed to customs and immigration officials in 130 nations.

"A true citizen of the world," Bert Miuccio notes, who met Dr. Grundy two decades ago. Dr. Grundy was then working in the Soviet Union at a "day job" while helping Adventist Health System set up a dental clinic for people affected by Chernobyl. It was one of his many altruistic endeavors over the years.

Dr. Grundy relates the story of his "fan club" in China. He was relaxing upon arrival in the lounge at the Intercontinental Hotel in Hong Kong after a few weeks in China.

"A Chinese gentleman kept staring at me. So, since I never meet a stranger, I walked over and asked him from where he is visiting."

"He said he was visiting from Xian, China. And then he said, in his best English, 'You're Paul Grundy, the PCMH godfather…' "

" ' Paul, I watch every video you have ever done. There are 37. I have found them on YouTube, which I can only watch when I am outside of China' ."

" 'Paul, you have huge secret fan club in the China primary care community. Many of the papers you have done and the videos have been reprogrammed on the Chinese equivalent of You Tube by me and my primary care friends' ."

Like America, China looks to enact some version of health care reform. It does so in part because, like the U.S., it faces a shortage of primary care providers in rural areas.

And in another similarity, the "Paul Grundy Fan Club" is growing in America, too.

Everywhere I go, more and more people know of this quiet and resourceful IBM physician. Where innovative experiments related to primary care are being undertaken, there is an awareness and deep appreciation for Dr. Paul Grundy, usually because he was there in the formative days, behind the scenes, quietly helping make things happen.

AMERICA'S CHAMPIONS OF PRIMARY CARE

"The way people think about health care has a lot of universality to it. It crosses cultures. People place a very high value on access to and receipt of health services. It may not be so universal that people are actively engaged in understanding what their risk factors are and are doing things for themselves — that's a challenge we face.

But people value health, people value access, people value receiving health care, people value relationships in health care. It has been quite striking to me how important the relationship between the individual receiving care and the person delivering the care is. What people understand and what they are willing to do is greatly influenced by that interaction."

— **Martin Sepúlveda, MD, FACP**, IBM, IBM Fellow, Vice President of Healthcare Industries Research

CHAPTER 17

PRIMARY CARE PHYSICIANS ADOPTING TEAM CARE

The Stakes Are Very High

T he *medical home* model can be challenging, especially to doctors who are resistant to change, and set in their ways. And that description takes in quite a few individuals who are practicing medicine.

The premise of this book, the reason I left a very gratifying career, and the reason we have assembled an outstanding training team is the fear that if we do not change how we do things as primary care physicians, the medical field itself and the many health advantages it holds for virtually everyone will be greatly diminished.

Experience over the past several years indicates that *Family Team Care* training results in a 35-80% increase in the number of patients seen every day. It also results in primary doctors enjoying a better work-life balance and far greater access for patients who don't have to take primary care health concerns into the Emergency Room or Urgent Care.

And it prepares the physician practice to make it possible to take the next step to become a *medical home.*

In 2013, the PCPCC published *The Primary Care Consensus: A Comparison of Health System Transformation Proposals*, a summary of the policy recommendations from the Partnership for Sustainable Healthcare, The Brookings Institution, the Bipartisan Policy Center, The Commonwealth Fund, and the Center for American Progress.

"Our analysis reveals an unwavering consensus across the health care marketplace and political spectrum that patient-centered, coordinated, team-based primary care is critical to achieving a high-value health care system."

Most primary care doctors see around 22-23 patients a day. The significant increase in people with health care coverage and the ongoing expansion of the Medicare ranks means that we will be asked to almost double that. Just adding more providers without a careful realignment of tasks will not save anyone any money nor would it necessarily improve the patient's experience.

eliminating the danger of a physician shortage

But through a true, well-planned re-engineering of primary care delivery, we may help balance out the convergence of more patients and fewer physicians. At the same time patients will maintain access to care, including those with chronic conditions, while fewer doctors will retire early because the benefits inherent with the *inside the exam room* team care model — in support of the *medical home* — holds the potential to bring back the joy of practicing medicine.

"…this book carries a message that combines hope with practical advice"

In the face of rising water, most people don't want to challenge Michael Phelps in a 400-meter freestyle event. They just want to be assured that they won't drown.

Because the one thing they can't imagine doing is swimming any faster.

By conveying that the model exists to help primary care practices survive — and even thrive in — the perfect storm, this book carries a message that combines hope with practical advice.

The notion of saving America's primary care physicians is the goal.

"…a proven and tested solution"

We believe that *Family Team Care* is a solid opportunity to adopt a proven and tested solution to the problems inherent in the changes to come. We present the model as a logical business tool that holds the potential for a quick return on investment and a systemic response that views health care reform as an ongoing process rather than an event.

We hope The *Familiar Physician —Saving Your Doctor in the Era of Obamacare* becomes a guide, showing a pathway to success that takes a positive, confident look at why primary care practices need to take advantage of the opportunities ahead.

Paul Grundy, MD sums it up, speaking of the motivation of IBM in changing the way they do business with health care providers.

"Tools like IBM's Watson are going to do for the doctors' minds what x-rays have done for our vision. New tools are coming."

"Formally, here's what we want," he notes.

"We want to drive the transformation to a patient-centered care model that promotes access and coordination across the continuum — a system that promotes prevention and wellness by collaborating with primary care physicians in ways that allow them to successfully manage the health of their patients and thrive in a value-based reimbursement environment."

"thus endeth the era of providers being compensated in a system that incents the wrong things"

"We will be funding three things," Dr. Grundy states. And from his perspective of providing guidance to over 1,000 health care organizations in America, we are listening carefully:

Those areas Dr. Grundy believes are worthy of our attention and our funding are:

- The change from episodic practice to management of patients with a team
- How payors pay and pay against outcomes
- Incenting patients to be empowered in their care

Thus endeth the era of providers being compensated in a system that incents the wrong things.

What we hoped and what we later proved beyond a shadow of a doubt is that by instituting reforms in their individual practices to streamline operations, elevate nurses and escape their time trap, primary care providers can reclaim their place as the *Familiar Physician*, the first and best source for health care for the vast majority of Americans.

As we have seen, this transformation allows the physician to spend more focused time with patients and also allows more quality appointments to be fitted into the schedule because the physician spends less time doing administrative work or clinical work that other staff can perform.

A *Familiar Physician* gives the best care in terms of quality and cost effectiveness.

Seeing the same patients on a regular basis enables *Familiar Physician*s to understand, not just read about, their problems and enjoy their trust. Because *Familiar Physician*s have an established relationship with their patients, the costs for the care provided are generally reduced across the board. For example, the patients of a *Familiar Physician* are less likely to visit the emergency room for routine problems. Also, the physician is less likely to order unnecessary tests; both are major reasons health care costs in our country are out of control.

Dr. Grundy's formal description of a *medical home* demonstrates how well the *inside the exam room* team care model fits into the future model.

"...shift away from an episode of care"

"It's a delivery system shift away from an episode of care towards managing the population. This is real stuff. This is real lives. This is simple. It's not rocket science. This is having the discipline to follow up, to follow through. We don't want a network anymore that is not managing the population."

*Familiar Physician*s provide more fulfilling care for all parties at the primary care level. Patients receive higher-quality, more efficient care. Nurses are more fulfilled working at the top of their license. Doctors experience less burnout and more job satisfaction. Health care organizations and insurance companies see costs reduced.

Just think about the 30-40 million patients now having insurance for the first time. They will not be going to the emergency room for every illness. They will have an accessible primary care doctor. Immediately, tremendous waste is eliminated.

greater patient access eliminating ER visits

During Dr. Grundy's address at the 2012 First Annual Innovations in Health Care Awards, he speaks of eliminating unneeded ER visits.

"I visited a *medical home* that the Army built in Savannah, Georgia, which has eliminated 95% of the encounters against the local emergency room because they have access 24-7."

My training team is proud to have brought our *Family Team Care* training to the Army outside of Savannah at Ft. Stewart. The training we carried out there brought quite a few other benefits to the ambulatory care setting there in addition to the significant reduction in ER visits.

Yet this one factor, minimizing expensive and unfamiliar care in emergency rooms and trauma centers, and then subsequently providing more in office care, clearly demonstrates the continuing approach of the perfect storm on primary care doctors.

Just as primary care physicians see more and more patients, the per patient reimbursement for these growing numbers will not be rising and may, in fact, be reduced. So medical practices that have not embraced a strategy like *inside the exam room* team care will be strained to the point of breaking.

The good news on that front is that more and more health care consultants and national leaders like Dr. Grundy are championing various forms of team care for primary care providers.

the value of "team"

Dr. Grundy describes the importance of a team care model to the assembly for his recognition by Blue Cross and Blue Shield of North Dakota.

"Remember the U.S. Olympic basketball team, composed of the greatest players in the world, who got whipped by Argentina, Yugoslavia and Spain? They were great individual players, but never came together as a team. This is what is needed in medicine. "

My own depiction of the value of "team" centers on trucks. During presentations I pick up a marker, go to the easel and draw a pickup truck.

The pickup truck represents most physician practices. You can barely get the current patients into this vehicle now.

I then draw a picture of an 18-wheeler, easily three or four times the size of the pickup.

With the coming wave of new patients under the ACA, we're going to need an 18-wheeler to handle the caseload we will have to take to reach or maintain viability let alone financial success. The concept is easy to follow, but how do you change a pickup into an 18-wheeler? If we can make this transformation, the future is bright for primary care and our overall health care system and the people it serves.

Obviously, the engine is the critical issue and must be increased in power in order for the 18-wheeler to take to the road. If you leave the old engine in place, it isn't going to pull the trailer. It may look like an 18-wheeler on the outside, but without a 600 plus horsepower diesel engine that also has 1200 plus foot pounds of torque; it still is going to perform like a pickup when it comes to pulling the load.

So, the physician is the engine of the practice.

adding horsepower

Additional horsepower comes from adding key staff members and from re-engineering the flow of energy. The result is a system that works efficiently for everyone.

Critical to the Patient-Centered Medical Home is a way to effectively change out the engine of this vehicle and quickly.

Of course, it's always easier to remain on the level of metaphor and draw pictures of pickups and 18-wheelers. It's a lot harder to make the changes in the land of reality.

The scope of transformation needed now is just as extensive—and with a lot more moving parts — as the change we went through in the 1930's and 1940's when our health care delivery model switched from the house call to the office visit.

The harried professionals in these contemporary physician offices generally need some refresher training on what makes a good team and what constitutes effective communication, along with some leadership tips for the team captain, the physician.

They need some coaching on how to integrate the electronic medical record into this new way of practicing primary care.

The *Family Team Care* approach brings this training together and along with the ability to see more patients efficiently, becomes a particularly solid resource for the successful management of chronic diseases.

AMERICA'S CHAMPIONS OF PRIMARY CARE

"Patients need to be at the center in a long-term comprehensive healing relationship with a personal physician, empowered with the right tools and linked to their care team."

— **Paul Grundy, MD**

CHAPTER 18

THE *FAMILIAR PHYSICIAN*
I Have To Get This Message Out

America's medical care is being fundamentally re-organized

Dr. Robert D. Reischauer, an economist and nationally recognized expert on health reform, Medicare and the federal budget made a prediction about health care reform when it was still pending legislation. "There is going to be," he said, "a long period of great expectations and very modest deliveries."

He might have added that there is also going to be a period of uncertainty for both health care providers and consumers. As you might expect, physicians think a lot about how reform will impact their practices. Everyone else wonders how it will affect their family, their business, their costs and their health.

So we're sure to have a time of uncertainty and it's likely to take years for the needed reforms to the way we deliver and pay for medical care to mature. In that time extending health care coverage and making care delivery more accessible and affordable is probably going to look like some combination of "the Good, the Bad and the Ugly."

But at the same time, the time period involved in the maturation of health reform will also provide an opportunity to adjust, to educate ourselves and to determine our options.

The good news underlying all of the existing and impending changes is that the *medical home* model rests at the core of them. For that reason my hope and my expectation is that the future of medicine, as long as it's anchored in robust primary care, is on solid footing.

"…it's about what the consumer really wants but too often doesn't get right now"

Dr. Paul Grundy affirms his belief in the "patient-centered" component of the *medical home* and offers American health care consumers something to look forward to over time.

"It's simple really. It's about what the consumer really wants but too often doesn't get right now. When you talk with consumers they tell you they don't have access, they can't get into see their doctors when they think they need to, and the doctor does not always communicate effectively — plus there's no real coordination of care."

"They would love to do something as easy and convenient as send an email and ask 'what does that lab result mean?' and get a clear answer in a reasonable period of time."

"They would love to have a much less painful experience when it comes to getting a prescription renewed, getting a referral or any number of other needs that may get put on a back burner by the physician's need to see 40 patients that day.

They would like to get simple reminders about their care as straightforward and reliable as those they get for their car or their cat."

Dr. Grundy adds, "The big shift we will see is on the service level. Like any other enterprise built around its customers everything will no longer be centered on making it easy for the doctor and not the consumer."

But while the new model of care will be patient-centered, the needs of the physician won't be sacrificed.

One of the core concepts of the *medical home* is to shelter primary care doctors from the perfect storm we described a little earlier in this book. The *medical home* and its emphasis on coordinated care will also play a role in the Accountable Care Organizations — what some people refer to, in its role as an extension of the *medical home*, as the "medical neighborhood."

Basically, an ACO is a network of health care providers and sometimes payors that takes on a shared responsibility for delivering care to a specific group of patients. Initially the ACO was intended for Medicare beneficiaries but it's already being directed toward the privately insured, too. If the ACO model is successful I would expect it to expand even more.

Along with being connected on a clinical level, the ACO participants are linked legally and financially in that they all take on the risks and potential rewards of the services they provide. The ACO can be made up of individual organizations like hospital systems, large physician practices and insurance companies and can include any number of providers such as hospitals, physicians, emergency departments or home health agencies.

Parts of how an ACO works, including the whole idea of aligning the incentives of the different participants, sounds a little like the HMOs of the past, a connection that could scare off providers and consumers who have bad memories about the weak points of HMOs.

But there are some real differences between the HMOs of the past and the ACO. One of the most important is the fact that ACO patients aren't limited to their specific network for their care.

From a structural standpoint, the ACO still operates on the basic framework of a fee-for-service organization but with stronger incentives to decrease costs, increase the quality of care and improve overall health — the "Triple Aim" we looked at earlier.

Although as I mentioned, the ACOs will vary in their component parts, the number of provider participants and the number of patients they reach, what they all share in common is the need for a strong primary care base.

The Patient-Centered Primary Care Collaborative estimates that, at this writing, there are nearly 10,000 *medical home* practices in the U.S. so the movement toward continuous, comprehensive care, coordinated by your personal care team is already underway.

What I would remind health care consumers and providers alike is that the transition from a standard practice to a true Patient-Centered Medical Home is necessary but not always easy.

We've talked about the numerous state and military innovation laboratories testing the *medical home* model across America. As I mentioned, they've been exceptionally gratified with the results. But at the same time,

THAT WAS THEN, THIS IS NOW

Courtesy of F. Daniel Duffy, MD, MACP, Senior Associate Dean for Academic Programs, Oklahoma University College of Medicine School of Community Medicine.

Medical need	That was then	This is now (or coming soon)
Appointments	"We can fit you in but you have to wait three days."	Same-day attention for acute illness.
Sick or injured at an inconvenient hour	Go to urgent-care center or emergency room to see someone who does not know your history.	Clear arrangement for after-hours care. Your medical history available electronically.
Prescription renewal	Call office and wait for doctor to return call.	Nurse handles immediately.
Preventive care	Remember to make appointments for checkups, screenings, and vaccines.	Electronic record tracks preventive measures and reminds you and the providers.
Test results	Play phone tag with the doctor.	Available at secure online portal.
Follow-up care	Up to you to make timely appointments.	Office tracks and reminds you of needed follow-up.
Specialist appointments	Specialists and primary care doctors may not effectively communicate.	Primary care physician coordinates closely with specialists.
Hospital release	Doctor has no idea you're in the hospital unless you initiate contact.	Knows when you are hospitalized and takes initiative to follow up.

they've found that conversion from the old to the new almost always creates a few challenges.

Some of the challenges are logistical, like putting in place the extensive technology needed to make the centers effective. Others are more intangible, including the requirement that doctors and other medical staff give up their old roles of operating in separate, independent silos and instead work within more collaborative teams creating a synergy that increases both capability and capacity.

"we don't have years to change"

A recent Health Affairs report forecasts that in order to be successful, practices will also need a "nurturing policy environment that sets reasonable expectations and time frames" and at least five years of various forms of external assistance to make the changes needed to become *medical homes* that eventually grow into "medical neighborhoods," an even broader network of providers that participate in the care of patients. The Accountable Care Organizations we discussed earlier are a good example.

While the projected timeline in the Health Affairs report may be a fairly accurate reflection of the large scope of the work to be done, I don't think we have that kind of time. In my own practice, using the *Family Team Care* training model we were seeing significant improvements in care management and coordination in a far shorter period — although practices can continue to improve as time goes on.

"encourage your doctor to move quickly to *inside the exam room* team care as a catalyst for building a successful *medical home*"

The fact is being in the path of a perfect storm doesn't give us the luxury of a lot of time to change. If you are a primary care provider the process has to be carried out as quickly as possible with no compromise in patient care.

If you are a health care consumer encourage your doctor to move quickly to *inside the exam room* team care as a good foundation for building a successful *medical home.*

"... the *Familiar Physician* to preserve what Americans love best about their medical care"

In my own experience, we were able to reclaim the pleasure of practicing medicine because everything improved: the quality of care, the efficiency of the office, staff morale, patient satisfaction and finances.

Beyond these obvious rewards moving toward the *Family Team Care* model is the best way to assure the continuation and in some cases, the re-birth, of the *Familiar Physician* to preserve what Americans love best about their medical care.

CHAPTER 19

ONE VOICE ACROSS COMMUNITIES OF CARE

Dan Pelino of IBM

O ver this past decade I have seen and been captivated by the passion and hard work that Dr. Sepúlveda and Dr. Grundy bring to making a meaningful change to our health care system. We all owe a huge debt to these crusaders and the support IBM gave them as we begin to reap the benefits of a stronger primary care health care system.

As a personal acknowledgment of that debt I will repeat an important moment in this book.

> "They didn't just rally a base of support. They rallied everyone. They didn't just rally doctors. They rallied large corporations, hospitals, pharmaceutical companies, politicians, federal officials, military medicine, Medicare, Medicaid, insurance companies, think tanks. Everybody.
>
> Drs. Martin Sepúlveda and Paul Grundy of IBM developed a strategy not to come up with the full shape of health care reform — only one vital piece.
>
> They came up with a platform that would enable good medicine to thrive. Just the platform. Then they began to champion that idea."

Now, with a very positive sense of déjà vu we can look at the next step that IBM is taking in an effort to help create a more viable health care future in America and around the world.

We got in touch with Daniel S. Pelino, General Manager, Global Public Sector, IBM Corporation to ask him about the evolving IBM vision for health.

In his current role, Dan Pelino leads IBM's business in the government, education, health care and life sciences industries helping its clients create smarter, more connected systems, while working closely with public and private sector organizations. He joined IBM in 1980.

Dan Pelino's team includes Dr. Paul Grundy, and he readily acknowledges the value of the efforts that he and others have already made.

"The work of Dr. Martin Sepúlveda and Dr. Paul Grundy as well as other leaders of American health care has helped establish a foundation for health care of the future," he notes, "and it's been an honor to see that work firsthand."

"Convene, collaborate and cross boundaries"

"I believe we can and should convene, collaborate and cross boundaries. Building on the work of Drs. Sepulveda and Grundy we can bring together many stakeholders around a common goal and develop one voice to drive individual wellness and community vitality," he adds.

Before I met Dr. Paul Grundy at a family practice conference, I had little knowledge about the scope of IBM's worldwide initiatives related to health care, life sciences and social programs. What I did know is that two-thirds of all the health plan information in the world travels across IBM infrastructure today. When it comes to electronic medical records, most of them are running on IBM technology. Advanced analytic solutions in genomics, cancer, and patient care and other areas come from IBM, too.

What this means is that organizations have to have something more than just IT strategies. They have to have a world view and equally important, they have to have the kind of people who are committed to it.

Because when you start to look at who provided some of the initial and ongoing leadership needed to transform primary care, it's IBM.

But what I believe, what makes it truly meaningful for me to do what I do is that as an enterprise, IBM is seeking not just to thrive as a corporation, but also to bring transformational change to our world.

here comes IBM… where we go from here

Dan Pelino shared with us some of the ways that IBM continues, as he referenced earlier, to convene, collaborate and cross boundaries.

"We have seen people and cities around the world use health care as a cornerstone, as a way in which they can redefine themselves and their communities. The link between the health and wellness of individuals and the economic and social vitality of the communities in which they live is unmistakable. It seems clear that healthy, active individuals are more likely to be contributing members of their communities. This leads to unbelievable benefits, specifically around economic development."

The notion of "one voice across communities of care" can readily be seen by looking at Rochester, N.Y.

We spoke with Dan Pelino just after he had attended a meeting of the NorthStar Network, a knowledge partner for the greater Rochester (NY) area executives across the health care ecosystem. At this meeting the discussion focused on the dramatic turnaround in a region that once depended on a vibrant Kodak company for jobs and growth.

"they didn't just rally a base of support… they rallied everyone"

"Over the last six years, seven large employers in this community convened to establish a focused long-term view and make Rochester one of the healthiest communities in America," Dan notes.

"Collaboration ensued as the employers were joined by the education community, business and investment colleagues, not-for-profits, and government agencies to create a unified approach to regional economic development with health and wellness as a cornerstone. And it's paying off."

Similar to the crusade for the Patient-Centered Medical Home, the leaders drove toward a single platform and goal, in this case, around economic development. They collaborated across boundaries with "health" as the core to the strategy.

What Dan explains is that Rochester has enjoyed a long history of collaboration between employers and providers which continues today, leading to a unique combination of low cost, high quality, and easy access. This vital health care system has a strengthening effect on the local economy.

a community that regards health
as a defining benefit of living there

As a family physician, I have spent decades wishing away the competitive, uncooperative, and duplicative health care world and hoped instead for just this — a community that regards health as a defining benefit of living there.

In Rochester, NY, health has become a community unifier, just as the *medical home* has helped unify America's health care leaders.

Dan Pelino brought a message of congratulations that day to over 200 community leaders of Rochester. The near miracle of Rochester's drop to a 7% unemployment rate can be attributed strongly to the focus around health care as an economic engine, to lower health care costs and deliver the kind of quality care that attracts businesses and people.

"What the Rochester community has managed to do," he explained, "is to stay focused on five major areas of improvement, which include an integrated care delivery system, a better understanding of access to care, nutrition and wellness, the role of government and academia on jobs and needed education, especially in science, technology, engineering and mathematics (STEM)."

If we doubt the ability of a coalition of committed people to help fix a damaged health care system, and in the process, make an important contribution to the overall economy, we should take a close look at what these innovators in Rochester have accomplished:

- Health care costs in Rochester are among the lowest in the country
- Commercial insurance costs are 30% below the national average
- Medicare spending is 21% below the national average

IBM is helping to send the message that health care can be an economic driver. Leaders can help make their city more attractive for business and industry. And the most important beneficiary in all of this is the individual. A key to smarter health care is ensuring that individuals are not just passive participants, but rather, active, engaged and well-supported champions of their own wellness.

Stakeholders across communities of care are leveraging new sources of information and insights into lifestyle choices, social determinants and clinical factors to help improve outcomes and reduce costs. By focusing on individuals and populations, healthier communities are possible and living in one of them is a good thing.

"Building on this new foundation, with the individual at the center," Dan Pelino observes, "we are quickly moving from just providing information at the point of care to providing impact at the point of care."

"Technology such as IBM's Watson computer can learn, teach and assist more than we have ever been able to do in the past. Something as seemingly unrelated to health care as Watson's winning turn on Jeopardy signaled this new era," he notes, "and it helped us re-think our expectations. The era of computing initially began with a role of tabulating, then we went through an era of applied logic and scaling. Now we are entering an era of knowledge and insight."

"...fall in love with the question, not the answer"

"We live in a time when if we ask the right question, the information is out there to answer it. Will we be able to frame it correctly? Let's fall in love with the question, not the answer. This powerful ability to leverage information about individuals and populations and deliver insights that drive individualized care and population health has tremendous opportunity to change the face of health care," Dan Pelino observes.

And, he explains, "When a community embraces transformative potential by collaborating across the boundaries of health care, social programs and life sciences to improve health care delivery and affordability....and then you add a new understanding of the expanded points of care that may include community facilities, pharmacies, social services agencies, or work places and homes...this powerful combination of forces has a true and lasting impact at the point of care."

Dan Pelino and the IBM team are exhilarated with the progress of this new way of thinking about communities of care and the powerful ways that we're going to be able to meet individual and global population needs in the future. Health care, social programs and life sciences leaders are taking action now by driving the adoption of holistic, individualized, proactive and collaborative approaches to care that are changing lives around the world.

These leaders are helping to make the fundamental transformation to individual-centric care delivery by facilitating shared planning, optimizing processes and systems, and enabling seamless collaboration in the dynamic and rapidly evolving care marketplace.

"There is something very profound in front of us and it is happening around the globe, through Smarter Cities, communities, and regions," he adds.

And I couldn't agree more.

CHAPTER 20

PROTECTING THE FUTURE OF PRIMARY CARE

What You Can Do To Save the Familiar Physicians

You can help ... and you've already taken the first step

You've learned more about the journey of primary care medicine in America over the last decade. You have a better understanding of the different forces at play and most especially the converging threats to the kind of health care you and your family hope for and should expect.

we're close but we're not there yet

The fact is we are within reach of a powerful and meaningful change to the way we deliver health care and the way we pay for it as a society, as well as what we value as individuals with regard to outcomes.

But that change and the benefits it carries for care providers and consumers will take place only if primary care physicians re-invent their practices, a transformation that includes access to reliable technology, evidence-based care, the willingness to engage patients in new settings and the desire to embrace the concept of *inside the exam room* team care.

Simply put, it's doing things differently than we do now. It's making changes within a system that has sometimes resisted them.

The scope of this change and its far-reaching implications for all of us requires what the media, policy makers, pundits and opinion leaders often refer to as a "national conversation." I'm going to encourage you to have that conversation on a far smaller and more personal scale. Here's how:

Help pass the word to established primary care doctors that there is light at the end of what has seemed for many, a dark tunnel. For newer PCPs the message is that the light may be closer than they imagine to the *beginning* of the tunnel.

give this book to your doctor

In either case, these very busy physicians are hard to reach. But a book given to them by a caring patient is very likely to get their attention.

And why would you want to do this? Because you might just save your physician's career when he or she becomes more aware of the opportunities, the increased potential and the proven strategies that are now available for primary care doctors to lead an interdisciplinary clinical team in general and an *inside the exam room* team in particular.

> The *inside the exam room* team care approach is a great first step toward being able to become a *medical home*.

There are a large and growing number of recognized *medical home*s in America. It's an effective and obtainable practice model and one that is clearly supported by this *inside the exam room* team approach and its ability to free physicians from tasks that don't exclusively require their skills and training.

As part of the initiative for change, Dr. Paul Grundy notes, in a May 2013 op-ed for Health Affairs, "While I would not argue that primary care should be all things to all people, it should be designed to achieve much higher performance than it achieves currently. Such a redesign of primary care is possible today."

"However, he adds, "if primary care is not successful in its core tasks of prevention, wellness, and the care of common conditions including many chronic conditions, it will not be possible to reach the 'Triple Aim' objectives of improving the experience of care, improving the health of populations and reducing the per capita and total costs of care in the United States."

I feel confident, and I know Dr. Grundy shares that confidence, that the Patient-Centered Medical Home and the primary care practice re-design needed to achieve it — including this *inside the exam room* team approach — will play an important role in reaching the "Triple Aim."

please suspend your political passions and ideologies
when the future of primary care is at stake.

We can endlessly debate the awkwardness and occasional confusion inherent in the evolving regulations and direction of health care reform. But within the complexity that comes with any health policy change of this scale, and there have been only a few others of this magnitude, there remains the refreshingly simple act of letting your elected representatives know how important the *medical home* model, and the continued availability of *Familiar Physician*s, is to you and your family.

I believe that the vast majority of primary care physicians and the health care field in general are strong advocates for the *medical home*. I believe further that when consumers are informed about the *medical home*, and especially if they are involved by their physicians in developing and evaluating certain aspects of it, they too become powerful champions for one of health care's most important innovations for improving the patient experience.

I hope you will join me in the quest to transcend political and competitive interests in pursuit of this essential platform for future medical care. With your help, the creation of *medical home*s will become not only an idea whose time has come, but an idea that rapidly improves care and quality of life for you and our family.

The *medical home* came along just in time. Let's all get behind it.

THANK YOU !

A SPECIAL THANKS

Dr. Martin Sepúlveda, MD, FACP
IBM
IBM Fellow & VP, Healthcare Industries Research

The National Business Group on Health, a non-profit group of more than 280 large U.S. employers, awarded its 8th Annual Award for Excellence and Innovation in Value Purchasing to Martin Sepúlveda, MD, FACP, IBM Fellow & VP, Healthcare Industries Research.

The award, which recognizes Dr. Sepúlveda for his leadership and commitment to employee health, productivity and overall well being, was presented at the Business Group's annual Health Agenda Conference held in Washington, DC.

"Dr. Sepúlveda is truly one of the nation's great innovators and visionaries in corporate health, productivity and employee benefits, as well as a national leader in the promotion of primary care and patient safety," said Pamela Hymel, MD, MPH, FACOEM, Senior Director, Integrated Health, Corporate Medical Director, Cisco Systems, Inc., who serves on the Business Group Board of Directors' Award Committee.

Dr. Sepúlveda, who has been with IBM since 1985, earned a bachelor's degree in Latin American studies at Yale University and an MD and a master of public health degree at Harvard University.

He completed residencies at the University of California San Francisco and at the Centers for Disease Control in the Epidemic Intelligence Service and the National Institute for Occupational Safety and Health. He also completed a fellowship in internal medicine at the Carver College of Medicine at the University of Iowa.

Dr. Paul Grundy
Global Director of IBM Healthcare Transformation

**"The *medical home* has been
brewing in America for a decade.
It's about fixing a broken health care system."**

In this role, Dr. Grundy develops and executes strategies that support IBM's health care industry transformation initiatives.

An active social entrepreneur and speaker on global health care transformation, part of his work is directed towards shifting health care delivery around the world towards consumer-focused, primary care-based systems through the adoption of new philosophies, primary care pilot programs, new incentives systems, and the information technology required to implement such change.

He has traveled the world, examined the health care systems of many nations and returned to champion a new platform for America, which has been embodied in the health care reform now underway through the Affordable Care Act.

Dr. Grundy also founded and is President of the Patient-Centered Primary Care Collaborative (PCPCC), an advocacy group of over 1,000 stakeholder organizations, including employers, health plans, primary care professionals, technology firms, pharmaceutical companies, policymakers and consumer advocacy groups, all committed to advancing the Patient-Centered Medical Home and primary care physician as the foundation of the new American health care system.

He is also Adjunct Professor at the University of Utah Department of Family and Preventive Medicine. In his efforts to drive comprehensive, linked, and integrated health care and the concept of the Patient-Centered Medical Home, Dr. Grundy's work has been reported widely in the New York Times, BusinessWeek, The Economist, New England Journal of Medicine and newspapers, radio and television around the country.

In 2012, Dr. Grundy was elected to the Institute of Medicine, a widely recognized national resource for independent, scientifically informed analysis and recommendations on health issues. The Institute of Medicine (IOM) is an independent, non-profit organization that works outside of government to provide unbiased and authoritative advice to decision makers and the public. The IOM asks and answers the nation's most pressing questions about health and health care.

He also received the 2012 National Committee for Quality Assurance (NCQA) Health Quality Award. Dr. Grundy is also the Chair of Health Policy of the ERISA Industry Committee.

Dr. Paul Grundy has received extensive recognition, including the Department of State Superior Honor Award for his role related to the crisis surrounding the two attempted coups in Russia, Department of State Superior Honor Award for work done in opening up all the new embassies after the fall of the Soviet Union, and Department of State Superior Honor Award for work on the HIV/AIDS epidemic in Africa. He also received four Department of State Meritorious Service awards for outstanding performance in the Middle East and Africa. He received the Defense Superior Service Award for outstanding service addressing HIV/AIDS and The Defense Meritorious Service Medal.

Special Thanks to these members of the IBM Team for their support in making *The Familiar Physician* accurate and timely:

Dr. Paul Grundy
Dr. Martin Sepúlveda
Dan Pelino
Gina Sandon
Barbara Castro
Toni Dudek
Robyn Bennett
Vineeta Durani
Holli Haswell
Christine Douglass
Sean Hogan
Sue Caldwell
Rizwa Khaliq
Collette Cassano
Melody Jones

ACKNOWLEDGEMENTS

Special thanks to the leadership of the PCPCC for their steadfast guidance of American health care to the *medical home*

The Patient-Centered Primary Care Coalition
2013

Board Officers

David K. Nace, MD
Chairman
Vice President, Clinical Development, McKesson Corporation

Paul Grundy, MD, MPH, FACOEM
President
Global Director, Healthcare Transformation, IBM

Douglas Henley, MD, FAAP
Vice Chairman
Executive Vice President & Chief Executive Officer, American Academy of Family Physicians

Andrew Webber
Treasurer
President & Chief Executive Officer, National Business Coalition on Health

Members

Errol Alden, MD
Executive Director & CEO, American Academy of Pediatrics
John Crosby, JD
Executive Director, American Osteopathic Association

Susan Edgman-Levitan, PA-C
Executive Director, John D. Stoeckle Center for Primary Care Innovation at Mass General

Beverley H. Johnson
President & CEO, Institute for Patient and Family-Centered Care

Marci Nielsen, PhD, MPH
Chief Executive Officer, Patient-Centered Primary Care Collaborative

Harlan Levine, MD
Chief Executive Officer, City of Hope Medical Foundation

Steven E. Weinberger, MD, FACP
Executive Vice President & CEO, American College of Physicians

Special Thanks To

Michelle Shaljian
Director of Public Affairs
PCPCC

POSTLUDE ON *FAMILY TEAM CARE*
Saving America's Primary Care Doctors

The transformation to an *inside the exam room* team care model enables the physician to spend more focused time with patients and also allows more quality appointments to be fitted into the schedule because the physician spends less time doing administrative work.

A *Familiar Physician* gives the best care in terms of quality and cost effectiveness.

Seeing patients regularly, *Familiar Physician* have a deeper awareness of their health concerns and enjoy their trust.

There is also a direct relationship between the relationship established with *Familiar Physician*s and the cost of care. For example, patients are less likely to visit the emergency room for routine problems, and the physician is less likely to order unnecessary tests; both are major reasons why health care costs are out of control.

Because of the EMR, this team has the capability necessary to organize, continually update, and investigate an incredible amount of data that accompanies a large patient panel. We also know that the team process allows the EMR to be utilized to its full capacity, thereby enabling better patient care.

Our busy primary care practice made transformational changes that today form the core of our training of medical practices in major health systems across America.

Now we are helping hospital systems and medical groups convert their inefficient and unprofitable primary care offices into highly efficient and profitable entities.

This proven model is a basic element in the changes that will make the *medical home* concept work in this country.

I think including a full description of *Family Team Care* training is especially helpful to the providers who are reading this book.

on-site training is crucial

Many fine organizations are helping physicians' offices convert their practice to a team care model. One thing is absolutely certain — it is extremely difficult and slow to make this transformation without on-site training.

The practice-based *inside the exam room* care team we developed, and have refined over this past decade, functions inside the primary care "operating theater of performance," the exam room.

By having a clinical team member collect and document all of the patient's medical data, our doctors no longer touched the EMR during the patient visit. The physicians only review and sign off on chart documentation during appointment breaks or at the end of the day. We are able to devote full attention to the patient, and accomplish the exam room visit much more efficiently and competently.

The goal of creating our new business model emerged during the extensive amount of time we were using my office as a living laboratory for primary care. I did not set out to create a new business model. I was just trying to find a way out of chaos.

What is the training process?
tested for a decade

In March 2012, the American Board of Internal Medicine presented the results of a three-year research project on primary care successes. Our practice, with results spanning a 9-year period was among the 60 selected for study and one of the featured practices at the final presentation. It was gratifying to look around the room and see several of the other selected practice groups that had bought my original handbook and were using some form of the *Family Team Care* model.

Among the distinctive features of *Family Team Care* is that we developed the model in a living laboratory. Few of the business models being put forth for team care have been tested and measured as intensely in a fast-paced primary care practice environment within a large medical group setting. Not all are physician-developed.

Our experience during this process was that we would solve one problem and would create another. Each of these actions and reactions were dealt with in turn. What we learned was that even beyond our initial understanding and expectations, a patient visit is a very complex, personal and variable experience.

What evolves goes beyond the addition of staff to the practice model. That particular fix has been frequently tried and generally found wanting.

orchestration and choreography of the team

Ultimately, it's not the sheer number of people, it's the orchestration and choreography of the team members that makes *Family Team Care* such an effective practice model.

Despite the effort required and the need to break away from some entrenched positions, the results were even faster than we imagined. For example, we noticed right away that we could schedule more patients.

Then we noticed that the practice was gaining significantly in revenue.

Then we noticed that the nurses absolutely love the new way of practicing medicine. And then, our patient satisfaction scores went through the roof.

Patients are delighted by the additional attention to detail and the opportunity to hear the nurse reiterate their issues to the physician (and to contribute to that communication, when needed).

At the end of my full-time practice in 2010, 95% of patients said they were likely to return to the practice and 94.5 percent say they were satisfied with the manner of treatment. The fact that the practice provides same-day service for all urgent visits — starting every day with 12 to 18 urgent slots -- plays a big part in patient satisfaction.

greater staff satisfaction

Staff members who are trained to do more than move patients and take vital signs also express greater satisfaction with *inside the exam room* team care.

It took us about six months to work many of the processes out, and then another two or three years to solve all the other downstream issues that occurred as we found new solutions to free up my time for patient contact and care.

We call the final product *Family Team Care*.

So *Family Team Care* is just that — a new *inside the exam room* business model for the completion of a visit in the doctor's office.

"…there has never been a better time to be a primary care doctor…" and *Family Team Care* training is part of the reason why

The key idea with any business model is to focus on the "job," and the "job" to be accomplished is what any good marketing analysis should discover.

For primary care, the job that the physician and his or her staff need to accomplish is to see more patients and at the same time provide high quality medicine.

So what we have created is a practice environment that epitomizes the highest and best use of staffing, allowing providers to see over 50% more patients in a day, increasing revenues, yet at the same time providing the highest levels of quality care and allowing doctors and nurses to once again love what they do.

patients are seen the same day that they call

Because *Family Team Care* represents such an efficient method of executing the patient visit, patients are been seen on the same day they call, and the new organization of the office has eliminated unnecessary waits.

The *inside the exam room* team care approach enables the physician to do only what she or he has been trained to do, leaving other tasks in the hands of a highly trained, capable nurse or medical assistant, who we refer to as the Team Care Nurse or Team Care Assistant.

Six months after *Family Team Care* training
In Crestview, Kentucky,
the internal medicine doctors who adopted the model
increased their average patient visits per day
by 47 to 60 percent,
and were able to improve
their rates of same-day appointments,
in the case of one doctor, by more than 260 percent.
Quality time with the patient improved,
and so did everything else.

So we replace physician tasks with best and highest use of the nursing and medical assistant staff in the office. Again, the primary objective of *Family Team Care* is to assist primary care professionals in performing the part of a patient visit that does not directly require a physician's clinical expertise. The physician's focus can then be directed toward the components for which he or she has been specifically trained.

better quality physician time with patients

By allowing the doctor to see more cases and by enabling nurses to spend additional time to perform tasks that they are capable of with the patient, the process actually creates a more effective diagnosis and better documentation than either party working on their own.

This change in traditional patterns is necessitated by the growing demand for primary care practice services, a demand that providers simply can't meet under the old model.

The problem is clearly in evidence in walk-in clinics and emergency rooms, which are full of patients who could be readily seen and effectively treated in the primary care practice.

While I deeply miss most aspects of my own family practice, and continue to think of my patients and staff, I am balancing that pleasure and satisfaction by sharing the *inside the exam room* team care model with colleagues across the nation. It's a model that we fine-tuned for a decade in private practice. The on-site training it includes is carried out within the context of an active practice. And most important, it works. It takes a short time to get into the new rhythm but results are felt almost immediately.

the joy of practicing medicine

I have now trained many other providers to: (1) spend more time in each exam room visit focused on the patient and (2) be more available to see other patients on their panel.

As a result of the on-site training offices find that they can add 3-5 more patients a day within a short time. Within twelve months, they can be seeing up to 50%-60% more patients. By the end of the second year, they can scarcely imagine that they once worked under a different model.

I know our physicians are on the right track when I receive email like the one I recently received from a fellow physician who had just completed the training.

He described how for the first time in two years "I can go home at 5:00 and be with my family and all I have to do when I get home is play with my children." He did not have to look at any charts once he got home. His work was done for the day. Also he told us for the first time in two years, he did not have to go to the office on Saturday.

The story of the *Familiar Physician* is the story of the joy of practicing medicine.

Benefits of *Family Team Care*

Benefits our clients have reported include:

- Improved medical care
- Increased daily patient visits
- Enhanced patient satisfaction by shortening wait times and increasing availability
- Improved incidence and quality of patient education
- Decreased legal vulnerability through improved documentation
- Improved quality measures

DR. PETER ANDERSON AND *FAMILY TEAM CARE* IN THE NEWS

Health Data Management, December 11, 2012, Building a Firm Foundation for *Medical homes*

"The practice-based care team we developed, and have refined over these past nine years, functions inside the primary care 'operating theater of performance,' the exam room. By having a clinical team member collect and document all of the patient's medical data, I no longer touched the EMR during the patient visit. I only reviewed and signed off on chart documentation during appointment breaks or at the end of the day. I was able to devote my full attention to the patient, and accomplish the exam room visit much more efficiently and competently. I have now trained many other providers to: (1) spend less time in each exam room visit; and (2) be much more available to see other patients on their panel."

— **Dr. Peter Anderson**

- Increased physician income
- Decrease in physician hours worked
- Much happier spouses!

As of this writing, we have trained more than 300 provider teams as a growing number of innovative administrators and physicians are helping to direct their future by taking advantage of opportunities to improve their practices and their enjoyment of medicine. We are proud to offer that potential.

quality measures soar

Based on measures used by the National Committee for Quality Assurance (NCQA) Heart Stroke Recognition Program, the quality of care in my own practice, as well as my chart documentation, improved dramatically after the implementation of *Family Team Care.*

HEDIS is a tool used by more than 90% of America's health plans to measure performance on important dimensions of care and service.

In 2010, using the HEDIS evaluative criteria, we were at the national 90th percentile or above for 9 out of 9 categories of Diabetes Management and this was also true for Breast Cancer Screening, Hypertension Management, and Colorectal Cancer Screening.

rapid return on investment

We brought on some additional individuals with strong backgrounds in training, information systems and finance to join a team of existing trainers, some that worked in our medical practice. These highly experienced clinical and other professionals come on-site to create the highly individualized training that has continuously demonstrated continuously a return on investment within 12 months.

So we expect our clients to see a financial improvement in the same year we provide the *Family Team Care* training — a particular benefit for larger practices that are struggling with the bottom line of making a large primary care practice work from a business viewpoint.

In my own practice, in the first half of 2010, we averaged 600 patients per month (which is approximately 35%—40% greater than the average primary

DR. PETER ANDERSON AND
FAMILY TEAM CARE IN THE NEWS

Advance for Nurses February 22, 2013 new Primary Care Nursing Model '*Family Team Care*' concept keeps RNs in a primary provider's exam rooms longer, producing life- and practice-saving results.

By **Jolynn Tumolo**

" 'After becoming comfortable with the added duties and seeing the many benefits of (*Family Team Care*), I wonder why every office doesn't do this' ," said Cathi Pope, RN.

"A nurse at the practice for 26 years, Pope left her job a year ago, along with family physician Peter Anderson, MD, creator of the *Family Team Care* model. The two now dedicate their days to spreading the good news that healing is possible..."

DR. PETER ANDERSON AND
FAMILY TEAM CARE IN THE NEWS
USA TODAY, FEBRUARY 17, 2013

"We can provide better care for our patients and ensure the long-term viability of our industry by embracing the reforms that have been put in place rather than fighting them." — By Peter Anderson, MD

"The entire system's viability hinges on the ability of primary care providers to absorb not only 30-40 million new patients, but a huge increase in visits by existing patients who should have been seeing a family physician in the first place rather than going to a specialist or emergency room."

care doctor), and spent 40 to 44 hours each practice week, with five weeks paid time off per year. And in 2010, I was earning twice the income I made before *Family Team Care*.

reinvigorating the practice of medicine

So now my career is devoted to sharing what I learned. It's why we prepared this book — to send a message out to my profession that the future can look different. This practice model will improve quality of care, profitability, patient satisfaction, staff morale and patient outcomes while reinvigorating their relationship to their chosen field of medicine.

The perfect storm we talked about earlier is still on the horizon. But the shelter needed to survive it and thrive in the aftermath is already here in the form of an *inside the exam room* team care approach to primary care medicine and its support of the *medical home*.

Family Team Care™ Medical Practice Training

Team Care Medicine, our training company, has developed these products and services to train providers, nurses and administrators in the implementation and operation of *Family Team Care*.

Through our proven, patent-pending curriculum and approach to training, we will prepare the staff for a new and effective approach to primary care.

Step 1 — Take our Readiness Assessment

Step 2 — On-line web based Introductory Course

An on-line interactive training session (about 1 hour) available for each training candidate / participant.

Step 3 — On-Site Live Training:

On-site training is provided in up to three (8.5 hour) days in the form of an engaging and interactive workshop.

Step 4 — By-Your-Side Launch Support

Includes 4 hours of on-site support and coaching for each team at start-up location when teams begin seeing patients.

Step 5 — On-going Virtual Support and Follow Up

After initial launch, our trainers/coaches will return virtually to the practice locations and provide additional follow-up coaching and encouragement.

TEAM CARE MEDICINE — Course Syllabus

The purpose of the curriculum is help the provider rapidly develop a highly functional and pleasurable practice-based care team that the provider leads. The care team is the most important component of the Patient-Centered *Medical Home*.

The curriculum will start the team building and system re-design that will yield the benefits of improved documentation and quality of care, improved productivity and finances, and improved patient and clinical team satisfaction.

HANDBOOK OF TEAM CARE FOR 21ST CENTURY FAMILY MEDICINE:

This 288-page manual describes the *Family Team Care* approach and is a working companion for motivated and well trained RNs and LPNs and MAs. This handbook is the foundation of our curriculum.

Annual Support:

Support includes a 24-hour call back guarantee to answer questions and help you solve issues.

DR. PETER ANDERSON AND
FAMILY TEAM CARE IN THE NEWS

The Atlantic, February 5, 2013, To Love Medicine Again, Physicians Need to Delegate. How one primary care doctor developed a system to deliver better quality care to more patients.

—By **Lindsay Abrams**

"The system, said Anderson, allowed him to see significantly more patients — up to 40 daily — while simultaneously directing more attention at individuals. And from 2003, when he first implemented *inside the exam room* team care, to 2007, he reported approximately 40 percent increased income to his practice, along with improved records keeping and quality of care. "And I fell in love with medicine again," he told me.

"Ironically, Anderson left his practice to become a full-time consultant, and has since gone on to train about 200 military and civilian teams. In 2012, he trained the U.S. Army on (*inside the exam room*) team care under a $1 million contract. Six months after its implementation at St. Elizabeth Physicians in Kentucky, in one instance, the three doctors who adopted the model increased their average patient visits per day by 47 to 60 percent, and were able to improve their rates of same-day appointments, in the case of one doctor, to over 260 percent."

Team Care Medicine LLC

The *Familiar Physician*
**Saving Your Doctor
in the Era of Obamacare**
By
Peter B. Anderson, MD
With Bud Ramey and Tom Emswiller

For more information, or to schedule a webinar for your team

please contact
Team Care Medicine®
4300 Geo. Washington Hwy, Suite 200
Yorktown, VA 23692
John D. Harbaugh at (757) 650-5603
jharbaugh@teamcaremedicine.com

Or contact Dr. Anderson directly:
Peter Anderson, MD, President
Team Care Medicine, LLC
panderson@teamcaremedicine.com

We look forward to talking with you.

TEAM CARE MEDICINE, LLC

Peter B. Anderson —
Founder & President

Peter B. Anderson, MD completed his Medical Degree in 1978 at the University of Virginia School of Medicine in Charlottesville and his residency training at Riverside Regional Medical Center in Newport News, Virginia. Dr. Anderson was a solo practitioner for 12 years before joining Hilton Family Practice in 1994. Hilton Family Practice, located at 10852 Warwick Boulevard in Newport News, Virginia, is part of Riverside Medical Group, a network of more than 80 practice locations and 325 board-certified providers offering a variety of medical specialties throughout eastern Virginia.

While in practice, Dr. Anderson was a Clinical Assistant Professor of Family Medicine at the University of Virginia School of Medicine, and Assistant

215

Professor of Clinical Family and Community Medicine at Eastern Virginia Medical School in Norfolk, Virginia.

In 2003 Dr. Anderson introduced *Family Team Care*, a practice model that focuses on highest and most effective use of clinical staff. The results have been extraordinary. The *Family Team Care* approach has improved professional satisfaction with practice, quality of care, documentation and financial performance. It has increased patient visit volume while raising patient satisfaction. In 2009, due to the success of *Family Team Care*, Dr. Anderson applied for and was granted the first NCQA recognized PCMH medical practice in Virginia. In 2010, Dr. Anderson was contracted by the U.S. Army to train the clinical staff in 21 community-based primary care clinic (CBPCC) pilots around the country. Dr. Peter Anderson is a leading authority and expert on clinical practice operations. He holds the following additional credentials:

- Been in private primary care practice since 1982
- Met national 90% HEDIS benchmarks for excellence in December of 2010 for mammography rates, colorectal screening, hypertension management goals and all nine diabetic management goals
- Author of book *"Liberating the Family Physician"* in 2005
- National speaker on clinical practice operations efficiency and PCMH for Merck from 2010 to present (given 30—40 lectures/presentations on the clinical practice efficiencies and PCMH under this venue)
- Presentations at the national meeting of the American Academy of Family Physicians on the *Family Team Care* process in 2008 and 2009
- One of the expert panel members at the Brookings Institute in April 2009 on the topic of "Restoring Primary Care Infrastructure in the United States"
- Presentations at the national meeting of the American Medical Group Association on the *Family Team Care* process in 2008 and 2009
- National print and online articles about the *Family Team Care* process in Family Practice Management, Business Week Magazine, Nursing Advance Magazine and Medical Economics from 2007—2010, Healthcare Finance News, Healthdata Management, The Atlantic.com and USAToday.com in 2013.
- Advisory Panel for Multiple Chronic Conditions for the AMGA since 2010

- Awarded in November 2010, a primary training contract for the implementation of *Family Team Care* for the U.S. Army's MEDCOM's CBPCC pilot program to develop practice efficiencies and PCMH in these clinics
- To date has trained 16 of the 21 Army clinics in this pilot program leading to very successful launch of the *Family Team Care* model
- Has also trained at hospital systems across the USA, helping them implement *Family Team Care* pilots

Steve has over 25 years of corporate operations management, IT and software development experience, including 14 years in executive level positions. He has led teams of more than 115 people in multiple locations, including offshore. He has built and managed operating budgets of $15 million and capital spending budgets of $4 million. Steve has delivered many mission critical high impact corporate initiatives. He also has start-up experience. As Vice President in 2004, he built an entire IT organization and technical infrastructure for Spiegel Brands, Inc. a $450 million new company. Steve is experienced in building strategic business plans and in managing their successful implementation. Steve received his BBA degree in Management Information Systems from James Madison University.

Steve Moberg —
Senior Vice President

Since 1987 John has advised early stage health care and technology growth companies on capitalization and strategic issues. During his career, first as an investment banker then as a corporate finance consultant, John focused on fund raising and opportunities with early stage public and private companies. From 1987 to 1996 he managed more than 50 public offerings as the lead banker and then formed his consulting practice.

Ron is an entrepreneur with more than 20 years of experience in leading training and

John Harbaugh —
VP, Business Development

Ron Chapman —
VP, Training

consulting organizations. Services include leadership development for first-line, manager and executive levels, training trainers and curriculum developers, public presentations for associations and conferences, and management consulting services. Ron is a Past President of the Southeast VA Chapter of American Society for Training & Development (ASTD) and was one of the first in the nation to receive ASTD's Certified Professional for Learning and Performance (CPLP) designation.

Donna English
Medical Assistant, Hilton Family Practice
Donna has twenty years of experience as a medical assistant with extensive experience in the regional hospital, community clinic and family practice environments.

Catherine Pope, RN
Catherine has thirty-two years of experience as a registered nurse and a broad knowledge of health care ranging from pediatrics to geriatrics. She recently received the 30-year service award within the Riverside Health System and heads up our nursing division.

Karen Evans, RN
Registered Nurse, Hilton Family Practice
Karen Evans has 40 years of experience as a Registered Nurse and clinic manager in a Team Care and PCMH primary care private medical practice. She also has her MPA.

Joyce Yates, RN
Registered Nurse, Hilton Family Practice
Joyce Yates has 30 years of professional experience as a Registered Nurse with extensive knowledge and experience in the fields of OB/GYN, Medical-Surgical, and Family Practice nursing. Joyce has worked on Dr. Peter Anderson's nursing team for 27 years.

Assisting Dr. Peter Anderson With The *Familiar Physician*

The *Familiar Physician* is prepared with the help of Bud Ramey and Tom Emswiller, who each have decades of experience in health care and medical communications.

Bud Ramey is the 2010 Public Affairs Silver Anvil Award winner of the Public Relations Society of America—the highest public affairs recognition in the world. Bud has served in top health care public affairs roles for over forty years and worked closely with leading physicians and the delivery of quality care throughout that time. He has won over two dozen international awards for excellence in communications as well as national and regional humanitarian and community collaboration awards. Bud is the author of two other major books on America's culture.

No COLORS —100 Ways to Stop Gangs from Taking Away Our Communities by Bud Ramey and Bobby Kipper was internationally released by Morgan James Publishing on February 14, 2012.

No BULLIES — Solutions for Saving Our Children from Today's Bully is also available now at Amazon.com and Barnes and Noble. This work offers parents and youth leaders the clear information and tools needed to help navigate the dangerous epidemic of bullying in America.

He resides in Virginia and can be reached at **budramey4@gmail.com**.

Tom Emswiller received a Bachelor of Arts degree in English and Narrative writing from Duke University and a Master of Science in Broadcast Journalism from Boston University. After serving as a VISTA volunteer in Appalachia and later training volunteers in community organization, Tom worked as a copy writer for Young & Rubicam advertising.

Following the birth of his children he worked for a number of years as a free-lance writer, and then later joined the Medimetrix Group headquartered in Cleveland, OH with offices in Denver, CO and Boca Raton, FL. As a creative director managing a department specializing in health care education, policy dissemination, marketing and communications, he also helped design focus groups with consumers, physicians and health care administrators, including an extensive project with the Robert Wood Johnson Foundation.

After moving from Denver to San Jose, CA in 2006, Tom has worked as the sole proprietor of his own health care communications agency collaborating with colleagues all over the nation to develop education and marketing materials in all media.

He can be reached at **temswiller@gmail.com**.

Together, Bud Ramey and Tom Emswiller have received over 18 international awards for excellence in communications arts, including one award placing their work as a Telly Gold "top 20 in the last 25 years" of filmmaking.

BIBLIOGRAPHY

American Academy of Pediatrics, "The Medical home"
  Medical home Initiatives for Children With Special Needs Project
  Advisory Committee, *PEDIATRICS*, Vol. 110 No. 1 July 1, 2002,
  pp. 184 -186, http://www.http://pediatrics.aappublications.org/
  content/110/1/184.full.

American College of Physicians, *The Advanced Medical Home: A Patient-
  Centered Physician-Guided Model of Health Care*, Philadelphia: American
  College of Physicians; 2005: Position Paper, (Available from American
  College of Physicians, 190 N. Independence Mall West, Philadelphia, PA
  19106).

American Hospital Association, 2010 Committee on Research, *AHA Research
  Synthesis Report: Patient-Centered Medical Home (PCMH)*, Chicago:
  American Hospital Association, 2010.

Thomas Bodenheimer, *Clinica Family Health Services, Primary Care Insight*,
  2011, http://www.primarycareprogress.org/insight.

Thomas Bodenheimer and B.Y Laing, "The teamlet model of primary care,"
  Annals of Family Medicine, 2007; 5:457-461.

Thomas Bodenheimer, and David West, "Low-Cost Lessons from Grand
  Junction, Colorado," *New England Journal of Medicine* 2010; 363:1391-
  1393 October 7, 2010, http://www.nejm.org/doi/full/10.1056/
  NEJMp1008450.

Yair Elbaz, Carlos Angrisano, Diana Farrell, Lucia Fiorito, Nicolaus Henke,
  Kamiar Khajavi, Bob Kocher, Martha Laboissiere, Alison Loat, Paul

Mango, David Nuzum, Jürgen Wettke, *A framework to guide healthcare system reform*, October 2006, http://www.mckinsey.com/insights/health_systems/a_framework_to_guide_health_care_system_reform.

Ted Epperly, *Fractured: America's broken health care system and what we must do to heal it,"* Sterling & Ross Publishers, 2012.

Health2Resources and the Milbank Memorial Fund, *"Better to Best" Value Driving Elements of the Patient-Centered Medical Home and Accountable Care Organizations*, March 2011 Washington, DC, sponsored by The Commonwealth Fund, Dartmouth Institute for Health Policy and Clinical Practice and the Patient-Centered Primary Care Collaborative, http://www.pcpcc.net/sites/default/files/media/better_best_guide_full_2011.pdf.

Ardis Dee Hoven, "A message to all physicians, chair of the AMA Board of Trustees," http://www.ama-assn.org/amednews/2010/09/20/edca0920.htm.

Ardis Dee Hoven, and LN, Dyrbye, "Physician burnout: a potential threat to successful health care reform," *JAMA* 2011; 305: 2009-2010. AMA Leader Commentary, Sept. 20, 2010, http://www.ama-assn.org/amednews/site/bio.htm#hoven.

IBM, 2005, *Healthcare Reform and IBM*, http://www.ibm.com/ibm/responsibility/employees_healthcare_reform.shtml.

K. Grumbach and T. Bodenheimer, "A primary care home for Americans: putting the house in order," *JAMA* 2002; 288: 889-893.

B.E. Landon, J.D. Reschovsky, H.H. Pham and D. Blumenthal, "Leaving medicine: the consequences of physician dissatisfaction," *Medical Care 2006*; 44: 234—242.

C. Ledue, "Pilot shows PCMH for primary care can reduce admissions, costs" *Health Care Finance News*, September 11, 2008.

What is a Medical Home? Agency for Healthcare Research & Quality: http://pcmh.ahrq.gov/portal/server.pt/community/pcmh__home/1483/what_is_pcmh_.

Ephraim Schwartz, "DoD and VA pursue PCMH model," *Government Health IT*, October 31, 2011, http://www.govhealthit.com/news/dod-and-va-pursue-pcmh-model.

M. J. Sepúlveda, T. Bodenheimer, and P. Grundy, "Primary Care: Can It Solve Employers' Health Care Dilemma?," *Health Affairs*, Jan./Feb. 2008 27(1): 151—158.

C. Sia, T.F. Tonniges, E. Osterhus, S. Taba, "History of the Medical Home Concept" (May 2004), Pediatrics 113 (5 Suppl): 1473—8. PMID 15121914,http://pediatrics.aappublications.org/content/113/Supplement_4/1473.long.

U.S. Dept. of Health and Human Services, AHRQ, 2012. *Patient-Centered Medical Home Resource Center*, http://pcmh.ahrq.gov/portal/server.pt/community/pcmh__home/1483/pcmh_home_v2.

ENDNOTES

A Dedicated Family Doctor Toils Late into the Night -
Big Blue Awakens a Nation

Brian Schilling, The Commonwealth Fund, Purchasing High Performance:
   What Is the Patient-Centered *Medical Home*? http://www.
   commonwealthfund.org/Newsletters/Purchasing-High-Performance/2009/
   November-3-2009/Featured-Articles/What-is-the-Patient-Centered-
   Medical-Home.aspx, accessed May 25, 2013.

Anne C. Beal, MD, MPH, Michelle M. Doty, PhD., Susan E. Hernandez,
   Katherine K. Shea, and Karen Davis, PhD., Editor: Martha Hostetter.
   Closing the Divide: How *Medical Home*s Promote Equity in
   Health Care—Results from the Commonwealth Fund 2006 Health Care
   Quality Survey
   June 27, 2007, Volume 62.

Chapter 1
The Sky Is Falling
A Grand Experiment Begins

National Academy of Sciences, Americans Have Worse Health Than People
   in Other High-Income Countries, January 9, 2013, http://www8.
   nationalacademies.org/onpinews/newsitem.aspx?RecordID=13497.

Massachusetts Medical Society, Health Disadvantage Is Pervasive Across Age
   and Socio-Economic Groups, August 8, 2012, http://www.massmed.org/
   AM/Template.cfm?Section=Home6&TEMPLATE=/CM/ContentDisplay.
   cfm&CONTENTID=74723, accessed May 10, 2013.

Steve LeBlanc, Huffington Post, January 24, 2013, Massachusetts Health Care
   Law Serves As Blueprint For Other States, http://www.huffingtonpost.
   com/2013/01/24/massachusetts-health-care-law_n_2541472.html,
   accessed June 10, 2013.

Chapter 2
The Next Thousand Days
Re-inventing the Exam Room

Core Principles and Values of Effective Team-Based Health Care, Institutes of Medicine October 2012, http://www.iom.edu/~/media/Files/Perspectives-Files/2012/Discussion-Papers/VSRT-Team-Based-Care-Principles-Values. pdf, accessed June 10, 2013.

Centerpiece

Better to Best, Value Driving Elements of the Patient-Centered *Medical Home* and Accountable Care organizations, March 2011, http://www. medicalhomeexchange.com/images/pages/PatientCentered_bettertobest. pdf.

Surviving the Tempest

The Perfect Storm bearing down on primary care medicine

Robin M. Lloyd, M.P.A., and Michael K. Magill, MD, Focus on Primary Care, What if we thought of primary care clinics as important research http://healthsciences.utah.edu/innovation/algorithmsforinnovation/focus-on-primary-care.php#.UY5sWZWzAQQ, accessed May 25, 2013.

The Patient Protection and Affordable Care Act (PPACA)
Baby Boomers Surging into Physician Offices

The Senior Boom is Coming: Are Primary Care — Are Primary Care Physicians Ready? http://www.amsa.org/AMSA/Libraries/Committee_Docs/seniors.sflb.ashx., accessed May 25, 2013.

Longer Workdays, Reduced Reimbursement, Failing Practices

David M. Cutler, Karen Davis and Kristof Stremikis, The Impact of Health Reform on Health System Spending, Issue Brief, Center for American Progress, The Commonwealth Fund, http://www.commonwealthfund. org/~/media/Files/Publications/Issue%20Brief/2010/May/1405_Cutler_ impact_hlt_reform_on_hlt_sys_spending_ib_v4.pdf, accessed May 25, 2013.

The Pharmaceutical Revolution

Daniel J. DeNoon, WebMD Health News, The 10 Most Prescribed drugs, April 20, 2011, http://www.webMD.com/news/20110420/the-10-most-prescribed-drugs, accessed May 25, 2013.

World Health Organization, http://www.who.int/en/, accessed May 25, 2010.

Pessimism Numbs Innovation

Merritt Hawkins, The Physicians Foundation, A Survey of America's Physicians: Practice Patterns and Perspectives, http://www.physiciansfoundation.org/uploads/default/Physicians_Foundation_2012_Biennial_Survey.pdf.

Not Enough Young Physicians Are Choosing Primary Care

Kaiser Health News, Doctors Face Image problems; Patients Deal With Shortages, Are Urged To Question Care, November 13, 2009, http://www.kaiserhealthnews.org/Daily-Reports/2009/November/13/Doctor-Image-Issues.aspx.

Allan H. Goroll, Bloomberg, Doctor Shortage to Spur Delays, Crowded ERs in Health Overhaul, November 13, 2009, http://www.bloomberg.com/apps/news?pid=newsarchive&sid=aOd7mHLJIh Jc, accessed May 25, 2013.

Beverly Woo, MD, Primary Care — The Best Job in Medicine?

New England Journal of Medicine 355:864-866, August 31, 2006.

American College of Physicians, Who Supports the PCMH Model, http://www.acponline.org/running_practice/delivery_and_payment_models/pcmh/understanding/who.htm.

Better to Best, Value Driving Elements of the Patient-Centered *Medical Home* and Accountable Care organizations, March 2011, http://www.medicalhomeexchange.com/images/pages/PatientCentered_bettertobest.pdf.

Ever-Present Malpractice Threat

American Medical Association, Physician Practice Information Surveyhttp://www.ama-assn.org/ama/pub/physician-resources/solutions-managing-your-practice/coding-billing-insurance/the-resource-based-relative-value-scale/physician-practice-information-survey.page, accessed May 25, 2013.

Mark E. Crane, Medscape Today News, Six Top Malpractice Risks in Primary Care, September 14, 2010, http://www.medscape.com/viewarticle/728306.

TEDxMaastricht, Paul Grundy: Smarter healthcare by smarter use of data

TEDxConference,Youtube, http://www.youtube.com/watch?v=npc0PLcYyx,, accessed May 25, 2013.

Wave of Physician Retirements Coming

American Association of Medical Colleges, Fixing the Doctor Shortage, https://www.aamc.org/newsroom/presskits/physician_workforce/, accessed May 25, 2013.

Electronic Medical Record Stress

Chapter 3
Hope on the National Horizon
Here Comes IBM
American Academy of Family Physicians, May 4, 2006, Martin J. Sepúlveda, MD FACP presentation.

Chapter 4
Birth of the Coalition
Dr. Martin Sepúlveda and Dr. Paul Grundy Stage an Awkward Reunion
World Health Organization, The Rising Importance of Family Medicine, June 26, 2013, http://www.who.int/dg/speeches/2013/family_medicine_20130626/en/index.html

Michael Barr, MD, MBA and Jack Ginsburg, American College of Physicians, The Advanced *Medical home*: A Patient-Centered, Physician-Guided Model of Health Care, Philadelphia, http://www.acponline.org/advocacy/current_policy_papers/assets/adv_med.pdf.

American Academy of Family Physicians, AAFP, Future of Family Medicine Project, http://www.aafp.org/online/en/home/membership/initiatives/futurefamilymed.html, accessed May 25, 2013.

Donald M. Berwick, Thomas W. Nolan and John Whittington, Health Affairs, The Triple Aim: Care, Health and Cost, Volume 27, Number 3. Patient-Centered Primary Care Collaborative, http://www.pcpcc.net/about/medical-home The Seven *Joint Principles* of the Patient-Centered *Medical Home*, http://www.pcpcc.net/about/medical-home, accessed May 25, 2013.

Chapter 5
A National Campaign Begins —
Dr. Grundy Steps Up
What is a Medical Home? Agency for Healthcare Research & Quality:

http://pcmh.ahrq.gov/portal/server.pt/community/pcmh__home/1483/what_
   is_pcmh_.

American College of Physicians, Who Supports the PCMH Model, http://
   www.acponline.org/running_practice/delivery_and_payment_models/
   pcmh/understanding/who.htm.

PBS Frontline, Systems — Health Care Systems — the Four Basic Models,
   An excerpt from correspondent T.R. Reid's book The Healing of America:
   A Global Quest for Better, Cheaper, and Fairer Health Care, http://www.
   pbs.org/wgbh/pages/frontline/sickaroundtheworld/countries/models.html.

Chapter 6
A Dent in the Universe —
The Tipping Point Is Reached
Patient-Centered Primary Care Collaborative, http://www.pcpcc.net.

History of the *Medical Home* Concept, Pediatrics, Vol. 113, Supplement 4,
   May 1, 2004, pp. 1473 -1478.

Stephanie Bouchard, Healthcare Finance News, New healthcare roadmap
   could lead U.S. out of the "graveyard," March 30, 2011 http://www.
   healthcarefinancenews.com/news/new-healthcare-roadmap-could-lead-us-
   out-graveyard?page=0.

Hawaii American Academy of Pediatrics, http://www.hawaiiaap.org/pdfs/
   AAP%20Member%20Spotlight%20Article%20-%20Sia_HS%203%20
   2010_1_.pdf.

Wikipedia, Barbara Starfield, http://en.wikipedia.org/wiki/Barbara_Starfield.

Annals of Family Medicine, The Teamlet Model of Primary Care

Thomas Bodenheimer, MD and Brian Yoshio Laing, BS, http://www.
   annfammed.org/content/5/5/457.

Chapter 7
Meanwhile Our Team Assembles a New Model
Creating Shelter Against the Perfect Storm
Health Data Management, Building a Firm Foundation for *Medical Homes*,
   Dec 11, 2012, http://www.healthdatamanagement.com/blogs/patient-
   centered-medical-home-45383-1.html.

Chapter 8
Dr. Grundy Becomes the Voice of Possibility
What If Everyone Had a Medical Home?

Chapter 9
Transforming Medical Offices One Exam Room at a Time
On-site training Is What Works

Catherine Arnst, Business Week, July 6, 2009, The Family Doctor — A Remedy for Health-Care Costs? How making primary-care physician the center of America's health system could ease the burden, http://opb.msu. edu/ucfa/documents/TheFamilyDoctorARemedyforHealthCareCosts.pdf.

Chapter 10
The Military Health System Embraces the *Medical Home*
Dr. Paul Grundy and Navy CDR Kevin Dorrance, MD Take the Helm

CDR Kevin A. Dorrance, MC USN; LCDR Suneil Ramchandani, MC USN; MAJ Jeff LaRochelle, MC USA; Fred Mael, PhD; Sean Lynch, BS; Paul Grundy, MD, Protecting the Culture of a Patient-Centered *Medical Home*, Military Medicine, Volume 178, Issue 2, pages 153-158, ISSN: 0026-4075, DOI: http://dx.doi.org/10.7205/MILMED-D-12-00146.

United States Department of Defense: HA Policy 09-015. Policy Memorandum Implementation of the "Patient-Centered *Medical Home*" Model of Primary Care in MTFs. Washington, DC, Office of the Secretary of Defense (Health Affairs), 2009. Available at http://www. health.mil/libraries/HA_Policies_and_Guidelines/09-015.pdf.

CDR Kevin A. Dorrance, MC USN*; LCDR Suneil Ramchandani, MC USN; Nancy Neil, PhD; Harry Fisher, Leveraging the Military Health System as a Laboratory for Health Care Reform, Military Medicine, Volume 178, Issue 2, pages 142-145,

ISSN: 0026-4075, DOI, http://dx.doi.org/10.7205/MILMED-D-12-00168, ISSN: 0026-4075, DOI: http://dx.doi.org/10.7205/ MILMED-D-12-00168.

Peter Anderson, MD, and Marc D. Halley, MBA, A New Approach to Making Your Doctor-Nurse Team More Productive — With proper training and delegation, your team can see more patients, deliver better care and feel more satisfied at work, http://www.aafp.org/fpm/2008/0700/p35.html.

Chapter 11
Back to My Story
With a Thriving Practice, I Quit to Help the U.S. Army
Bob Kehoe, Hospital & Healthcare Networks, Transforming Care Delivery, http://www.hhnmag.com/hhnmag/jsp/articledisplay.

> jsp?dcrpath=HHNMAG/Article/data/05MAY2012/0512HHN_FEA_ interview&domain=HHNMAG.

Paul Grundy, MD, Bringing Knowledge Home, June 2012 Commentary published by the Institute of Medicine of the National Academies, Contributor to the Learning Health System Commentary Series of the IOM Roundtable on Value & Science-Driven Health Care, www.iom.edu/ learninghealthsystem.

Chapter 12
Bringing the *Medical home* to Federal Employees
LCDR Ramchadani Helps Harness the Power of the Federal Government
Eric W. Christensen, PhD; CDR Kevin A. Dorrance, MC USN; LCDR Suneil Ramchandani, MC USN; Sean Lynch, BS; Christine C. Whitmore, PhD; Amanda E. Borsky, MPP; CDR Linda G. Kimsey, MC USN; Linda M. Pikulin, MS; Thomas A. Bickett, MA, Impact of a Patient-Centered *Medical Home* on Access, Quality, and Cost, Military Medicine Volume 178, Issue 2, pages 135-141 ISSN: 0026-4075, DOI: http://dx.doi. org/10.7205/MILMED-D-12-00220.

Press Office, http://www.whitehouse.gov/the-press-office/white-house- appoints-2010-2011-class-white-house-fellows.

CAPT Mark L. Dick, MD, FACP, American College of Physicians, Governor's Newsletter, June 2012,

http://www.acponline.org/about_acp/chapters/navy/newsletter612.htm.

Chapter 13
Setting Strong Standards for the *Medical Home*
NCQA Takes the Lead
NCQA: The State of Health Care Quality 2009: Value, Variation, and Vulnerable Populations. Washington, DC, National Committee of Quality Assurance. Available at www.ncqa.org/Portals/0/Newsroom/ SOHC/SOHC_2009.pdf; accessed June 23, 2010.

National Committee for Quality Assurance, http://www.ncqa.

Building a Firm Foundation for *Medical Home*s, Health Data Management, http://www.healthdatamanagement.com/blogs/patient-centered-medical-home-45383-1.html.

Awards video for 2012 Health Quality Award of the NCQA http://www. youtube.com/watch?v=3QiNgjzxRyc.

Ken Terry, Medical Economics, Volume 84 Number 15, August 3, 2007, An effective way to use assistants — Training nurses and MAs to take histories and provide patient education boosts productivity, income, and quality of care, http://www.questia.com/library/1P3-1347597421/an-effective-way-to-use-assistants.

Patient-Centered Primary Care Collaborative, http://www.pcpcc.net.

Innovations in Health Care Awards — Dr. Paul Grundy, http://www.youtube. com/watch?v=Mfn_NHF264U.

Chapter 14
A Look at Medical home 2.0
Taking the First Step

San Diego Organization of Healthcare Leaders, http://sohl.ache.org/x263.xml.

Chapter 15
Empowering the Patient
The Third Leg of the Stool

A. Mark Fendrick, M.D, University of Michigan, Department of Internal Medicine and Health Management and Policy, Center for Value-Based Insurance Design, www.vbidcenter.org.

A. Mark Fendrick, MD, Bruce Sherman, MD and Dennis White, PCPCC and National Business Coalition on Health, Aligning Incentives and Systems, Promoting Synergy Between Value-Based Insurance Design and the Patient Centered *Medical home*,

http://www.sph.umich.edu/vbidcenter/registry/pdfs/whitepaper33010.pdf accessed June 24, 2013.

Chapter 16
The *Medical Home* Model Is Bringing Something Special
Success in Vermont

Vermont Blueprint for Health, 2012 Annual Report, http://hcr.vermont. gov/sites/hcr/files/Blueprint/Blueprint%20for%20Health%202012%20 Annual%20Report%20%2002_14_13_FINAL.pdf.

Keep Employers In a Primary Role: A Conversation With Martin Sepúlveda, MD, Managed Care, November 2008, http://www.managedcaremag.com/ archives/0811/0811.qna_Sepúlveda.html, accessed May 25, 2013.

Chapter 17
Primary Care Physicians Adopting Team Care
The Stakes Are Very High

Michelle Shaljian and Nikola Lojanica, PCPCC, The Primary Care Consensus: A Comparison of Health System Transformation Proposals, http://www.pcpcc.net/download/4168/Primary%20Care%20 Consensus%20v4%28print%29.pdf?redirect=node/5993, accessed June 24, 2013.

Paul Grundy, MD, The Healthcare Blog, Now you have healthcare data. So where does it go?

http://thehealthcareblog.com/blog/2012/01/27/now-you-have-healthcare-data-so-where-does-it-go/, accessed May 25, 2013.

Innovations in Health Care Awards — Dr. Paul Grundy, http://www.youtube. com/watch?v=Mfn_NHF264U.

Chapter 18
The *Familiar Physician*
I Have To Get This Message Out

The Associated Press, Health overhaul: Understanding the pros and cons, modified: November 28, 2009, published: November 28, 2009, http:// newsok.com/health-overhaul-understanding-the-pros-and-cons/article/ feed/111492, accessed May 25, 2013.

Paul A. Nutting, Benjamin F. Crabtree, William L. Miller, Kurt C. Stange, Elizabeth Stewart, and Carlos Jaén, NIH Public Access, Health Affairs, March 2011, Transforming Physician Practices To Patient-Centered *Medical Homes*: Lessons From The National Demonstration Project, http://www.ncbi.nlm.nih.gov/pmc/articles/PMC3140061/.

F. Daniel Duffy, MD, MACP, Senior Associate Dean for Academic Programs, Oklahoma University College of Medicine School of Community

Medicine. That was then this is now, courtesy of Dr. Duffy also published http://www.consumerreports.org/cro/magazine/2013/07/a-doctor-s-office-that-s-all-about-you/index.htm.

Chapter 19
One Voice Across Communities of Care
Dan Pelino of IBM

Healthy Cities, Rochester, NY, http://www.youtube.com/watch?v=rZUq3TjLsQI.

Greater Rochester NY Regional Economic Development, http://www.rochesterbiz.com/Data/Documents/Affordable%20health%20care%20brochure%20Final.pdf.

Chapter 20
Protecting the Future of Primary Care
What You Can Do To Save the Familiar Physicians

A Special Thanks

PR Newswire, http://www.prnewswire.com/news-releases-test/ibm-executive-dr-martin-Sepúlveda-wins-prestigious-national-business-group-on-health-award-87460507.html.

Innovations in Health Care Awards — Dr. Paul Grundy, http://www.youtube.com/watch?v=Mfn_NHF264U.

CPSIA information can be obtained at www.ICGtesting.com
Printed in the USA
BVOW02s0926260813

329547BV00002B/21/P